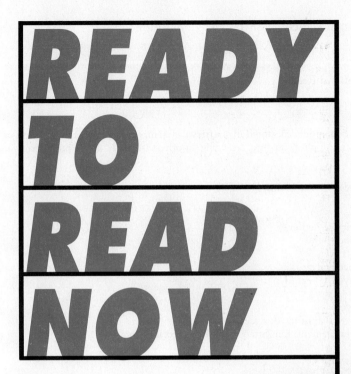

A Skills-Based Reader

Karen Blanchard

Christine Root

Longman

This book is dedicated to our students—past, present, and future.

Ready to Read Now: A Skills–Based Reader

Pearson Education, 10 Bank Street, White Plains, NY 10606

Executive editor: Laura Le Dréan
Senior development editor: Françoise Leffler
Project editor: Helen B. Ambrosio
Production coordinator: Melissa Leyva
Director of manufacturing: Patrice Fraccio
Senior manufacturing buyer: Dave Dickey
Cover design: Pat Wosczyk
Cover photo: April / Getty Images
Text design adaptation: Elm Street Publishing Services, Inc.
Text composition and project management: Elm Street Publishing Services, Inc.
Photo research: Dana Klinek
Photo and text credits appear on page vi.
Illustrations: José Luis Briseño, Peter Grau

Library of Congress Cataloging-in-Publication Data

Blanchard, Karen Lourie
  Ready to read now : a skills-based reader / by Karen Blanchard and Christine Root.
    p. cm.
   ISBN 0-13-177647-9
  1. English language—Textbooks for foreign speakers. 2. Reading—Problems, exercises, etc. 3. Readers.
I. Root, Christine Baker, 1945– II. Title.

PE1128.B5868 2005
428.6'4—dc22

2004008379

ISBN: 0-13-177647-9

LONGMAN ON THE **WEB**

Longman.com offers online resources for teachers and students. Access our Companion Websites, our online catalog, and our local offices around the world.

Visit us at **longman.com.**

Printed in the United States of America
10–V011–13

Contents

Scope and Sequence

CHAPTER	READING SKILLS	VOCABULARY SKILLS	MAIN READING	HAVE SOME FUN
1 Get the Picture	Identifying topics and main ideas	Using a dictionary—guidewords; multiple meanings	*It Happened by Accident*	Taking a survey Using charts
2 Take a Closer Look	Identifying details	Using a dictionary—parts of speech	*Unusual Fads of the 1920s*	Completing a crossword puzzle
3 Make Guesses	Previewing and predicting	Word parts: Prefixes	*Funny Business*	Reading jokes Taking a magazine quiz
4 Read Quickly	Skimming and scanning	Synonyms and antonyms	*Bear Necessities*	Taking a magazine quiz
5 Figure It Out	Using context clues	Definition clues Comparison clues Contrast clues Example clues	*Idioms and Proverbs*	Reading ads
6 Put Things in Order	Recognizing sequence	Word parts: Suffixes	*The Story of the Two Brothers*	Creating a folktale
7 Believe It or Not	Fact vs. opinion	Using word maps	*The Godfather: A Movie Classic*	Reading the entertainment section of a newspaper
8 Read between the Lines	Making inferences	Compound words	*Swimming Buddies*	Reading travel ads Writing a postcard

Credits

PHOTO CREDITS

Page 1. Printed by permission of the Norman Rockwell Family Agency. Copyright © 1960 the Norman Rockwell Family Entities, Norman Rockwell Art Collection Trust, The Norman Rockwell Museum at Stockbridge, Massachusetts.
Page 16. left: ©Corbis/Paul Steel. right: Copyright © 2003 Raytheon Company. All rights reserved.
Page 17. ©Corbis/Bettmann.
Page 19. top: ©Corbis/Bettmann. bottom: ©Corbis Sygma/Andanson James.
Page 29. Vincent van Gogh. 1853–1890. The Bedroom, 1889, oil on canvas, 73.6 × 92.3 cm. Helen Birch Bartlett Memorial Collection. 1926.417. Photograph by Greg Williams. Reproduction, The Art Institute of Chicago.
Page 38. left, right: ©Corbis/Bettmann.
Page 39. ©Corbis/Royalty-Free.
Page 44. ©Corbis/Bettmann.
Page 48. Paramount/Courtesy Everett Collection.
Page 55. Photograph © 2003 Museum of Fine Arts, Boston. Claude Monet, French, 1840–1926. *Grainstack (Sunset)*, 1891. Oil on canvas. 73.3 x 92.7 cm (28 $\frac{7}{8}$ × 36 $\frac{1}{2}$ in.). Museum of Fine Arts, Boston. Juliana Cheney Edwards Collection. 25.112.
Page 61. top left: ©Fuse/Thinkstock. bottom left: nigel hillier/Alamy. top right: Courtesy of Photofest. bottom right: Illustration by Peter Wallace. © 1999 National Geographic Society. All rights reserved.
Page 62. left: Illustration by Peter Wallace © 1999 National Geographic Society. All rights reserved. right: Photograph courtesy of Shooting Star.
Page 71. Funeral Procession, Ellis Wilson. Louisiana: Amistad Research Center–Aaron Douglas Collection, Tulane University, New Orleans.
Page 84. ©Corbis/John Conrad.
Page 92. Copyright 1997 by Randy Glasbergen.
Page 110. PEANUTS reprinted by permission of United Feature Syndicate, Inc.
Page 129. ©Corbis/Bob Krist.
Page 138. Paramount/Courtesy Everett Collection.
Page 149. Photograph © 2003 Museum of Fine Arts, Boston. John Singer Sargent, American, 1856–1925. *Mrs. Fiske Warren (Gretchen Osgood) and Her Daughter Rachel*, 1903. Oil on canvas. 152.4 × 102.55 cm (60 × 40 $\frac{3}{8}$ in.) Museum of Fine Arts, Boston. Gift of Mrs. Rachel Warren Barton and Emily L. Ainsley Fund; 64.693.
Page 158. ©Zena Holloway/SuperStock, Inc.
Page 167. top: Photo courtesy of Brigitte Alias. bottom: ©Index Stock Imagery/Royalty-Free.
Page 168. ©Corbis/David Samuel Robbins.

TEXT CREDITS

Page 28. Survey source: The Lemelson Foundation.
Page 60. Adapted from "Funny Business" by David George Gordon. *National Geographic Kids*, April 1999. © National Geographic Society.
Page 78. The Lewis and Clark Expedition
Page 84. Adapted from "Bear Necessities: How Polar Bears Survive the Deep Freeze" by Kathy Kranking. *National Geographic Kids*, December 2001. © 2001 National Geographic Society.
Page 102. Adapted from "Idioms and Proverbs." Fact Monster. © 2003 Family Education Network. 13 May, 2004 <http://www.factmonster.com/ipka/A0769301.html>.
Page 118. The Story of the Two Brothers: From FACES' May 2002 issue: Samoans, © 2002, Cobblestone Publishing, 30 Grove Street, Suite C, Peterborough, NH 03458. All Rights Reserved. Reprinted by permission of Carus Publishing Company.
Page 127. "Three Fish—A Tale from India retold by Heather Forest." © 2000 Heather Forest. Reprinted from Story Arts Online (http://www.storyarts.org).
Page 158. Adapted from "Swimming Buddies." *National Geographic Kids*, August 1999. © National Geographic Society.

Introduction

Like its companion series, *Ready to Write,* the **Ready to Read** series comprises three task-based, skill-building textbooks for students of English. Also like its sister series, the new series is skills-based and user-friendly, a series that both teachers and students will find easy to follow and use. **Ready to Read Now** is appropriate for use in both the United States and abroad, in academic preparatory or adult education settings, for professionals or students, and at secondary or university levels.

THE APPROACH

The books in the **Ready to Read** series are made up of task-based chapters, each of which has reading and vocabulary skill-building as its primary focus. In this series we started by choosing the reading and vocabulary skills we wanted to teach in each chapter and then selecting readings for their value in helping students understand and practice those specific skills.

As a skill is presented, paintings, photographs, graphics, examples, and short texts, both prose and nonprose, are used to illustrate that skill and provide practice. Each chapter opens with a pictorial representation of a reading skill to give students a non-verbal reference point. The reading skill is then practiced throughout the text and recycled and reinforced in every subsequent chapter. The intrinsic difficulty of each individual skill dictates whether it is a skill that is recycled throughout the series or introduced and practiced only in books two and/or three. For example, a foundational skill such as distinguishing main ideas from supporting details appears in all three books, while a skill such as skimming appears only in the later books.

Like the *Ready to Write* series, the exercises in the **Ready to Read** series involve the students actively. Proficient reading, like writing, requires a network of complex skills that can be taught, practiced, and improved. This series develops competency in these skills by taking students on a step-by-step progression through the reading skills and word-attack strategies that promote efficient and effective reading, and then by continuously recycling the practice of those skills. Students read with a purpose, be it to increase reading efficiency, summarize an article, apply the skill presented in the chapter at hand, or review those skills presented in previous chapters.

In addition to demonstrating comprehension through standard exercises, students work with visual representations of readings by completing a chart, graph, table, or outline to help them focus on the underlying structure of the reading and understand the interrelationships among ideas.

We hope you enjoy working through these activities with your students. At any level, they are definitely **Ready to Read Now!**

Acknowledgments

For their help in envisioning, supporting, and creating this book, we thank Laura Le Dréan, Françoise Leffler, Melissa Leyva, Dana Klinek, and Helen Ambrosio at Longman, as well as our friends, family, and colleagues: Barbara Alfond; Brigitte Alias; Daniel Blanchard; Mimi Braverman, Kathryn Costello; Diane Englund; Vicky and Ozzie Frankel; Vicky Goldstein; Jann Grutchfield; Candace Kerner; Sharon McKay; Lynn Meng; David, Matt, and Ian Root; Nancy Stevenson; Lisa Weinstein; and Carole Whittemore.

The visual arts play an important role in this book. For their help in directing us to just the right pictures, we thank Elliott Bostwick Davis and Gilian Shallcross at the Museum of Fine Arts, Boston.

CHAPTER 1

Get the Picture
Identifying Topics and Main Ideas

Look at the painting by Norman Rockwell, a well-known twentieth-century American artist. Discuss what you see with a partner. Then answer the question.

What is the painting about?
 a. a mirror
 b. the artist himself
 c. a pipe

When you looked at the painting, you decided what it was about. In other words, you identified the topic. This helped you understand the painting better. In the same way, identifying the topic of a reading will help you better understand the reading. It will also help you remember what you read.

Sharpen Your Reading Skills

IDENTIFYING TOPICS

Reading is a complex process, especially when you are reading something that is not in your native language. The first step to becoming a successful reader is identifying the topic of the passage. The next step is identifying the main idea. In this chapter you will learn how to identify both the topic and the main idea of a reading passage. Let's start with the first step: identifying the topic.

The subject of a movie or a conversation is called the **topic**. The subject of most writing is also called a topic. The topic answers the question, "What or who is it about?" The topic is usually just a word or a short phrase.

Identifying the Topic of a List

A. One word in each of the following lists answers the question, "What is this list about?" That word is the topic of the list. Circle the topic of each list.

Example

apple
(fruit)
pear
banana
orange

1. shirt	2. north	3. money	4. chair
dress	south	dollar	furniture
clothing	east	euro	sofa
pants	directions	pound	table
sweater	west	yen	bed

5. bracelet	6. sunny	7. square	8. ant
necklace	cloudy	shapes	beetle
ring	rainy	triangle	ladybug
earrings	weather	circle	bee
jewelry	cold	rectangle	insects

B. Write the topic of each of the following lists on the line. Ask yourself, "What is this list about?" The answer is the topic.

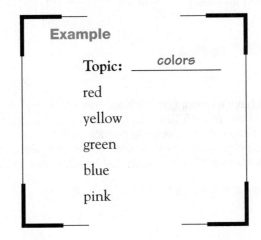

Example

Topic: ___colors___

red

yellow

green

blue

pink

1. Topic: _____

tennis

golf

horseback riding

soccer

swimming

2. Topic: _____

rock 'n' roll

jazz

classical

rap

New Age

3. Topic: _____

Mars

Jupiter

Earth

Venus

Pluto

4. Topic: _____

Nile

Amazon

Danube

Mississippi

Yangtze

5. Topic: _____

sheep

cows

donkeys

goats

horses

6. Topic: _____

teacher

plumber

secretary

chef

pilot

Identifying the Topic of an E-mail

C. The topic of an e-mail is written on the subject line. Write the topic of each of the following e-mails. Follow the example.

Example

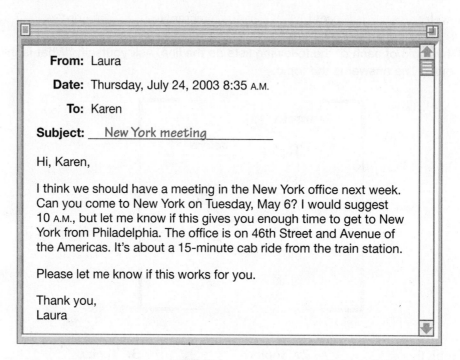

From: Laura

Date: Thursday, July 24, 2003 8:35 A.M.

To: Karen

Subject: _New York meeting_

Hi, Karen,

I think we should have a meeting in the New York office next week. Can you come to New York on Tuesday, May 6? I would suggest 10 A.M., but let me know if this gives you enough time to get to New York from Philadelphia. The office is on 46th Street and Avenue of the Americas. It's about a 15-minute cab ride from the train station.

Please let me know if this works for you.

Thank you,
Laura

1.

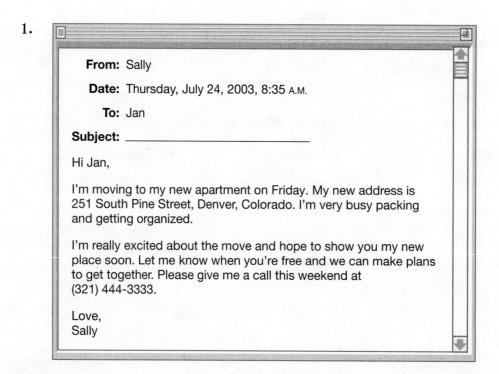

From: Sally

Date: Thursday, July 24, 2003, 8:35 A.M.

To: Jan

Subject: _____

Hi Jan,

I'm moving to my new apartment on Friday. My new address is 251 South Pine Street, Denver, Colorado. I'm very busy packing and getting organized.

I'm really excited about the move and hope to show you my new place soon. Let me know when you're free and we can make plans to get together. Please give me a call this weekend at (321) 444-3333.

Love,
Sally

2.

From: Sue

Date: Thursday, July 24, 2003 8:35 A.M.

To: Gerald

Subject: _____

Dear Gerald,

Thank you so much for the CD you sent me for my birthday. It's a great gift. I love jazz, and Billie Holiday is one of my favorite jazz singers. I took the CD in my car and listened to it all the way to work.

When I got to work, I was surprised to find that my co-workers had planned a birthday party for me. They even decorated the whole office with balloons.

Thanks again for remembering my birthday. Give my love to the kids.

Love,
Sue

3.

From: Marty

Date: Thursday, July 24, 2003 8:35 A.M.

To: Ruth

Subject: _____

Ruth,

Here are the directions to my house. Take the Hampshire Parkway north for 5 miles. Get off at the Franklin Street exit. Turn left at the end of the ramp and get on Walnut Ave. Stay on Walnut for about 2 miles. You'll go through three stoplights. At the fourth light, make a right onto Locust St. You'll see a gas station at the corner of Walnut and Locust. Go straight on Locust for two blocks. My house is in the middle of the second block on the right side of the street (number 542). It's a brick house with a green door.

See you around 7 tonight.
Marty

Identifying the Topic of a Paragraph

Most English writing is organized into groups of sentences called **paragraphs**. The sentences in a paragraph are related to each other because they are all about the same general topic. How do you identify the topic of a paragraph? One way is to look for a word or phrase that is often repeated. That word or phrase is often the topic. Another way is to pretend you have to tell a friend what you just read about using only one word or phrase. That word or phrase is the topic.

D. Identify the topic of each of the following paragraphs. Remember to ask yourself, "Who or what is the paragraph about?"

> ### Example
>
> Do you know the famous redhead Lucille Ball? She is one of the most-loved television and film actresses in American history. In fact, people all over the world can recognize her. Most people remember Lucille Ball best for her starring role in television's hit comedy called *I Love Lucy*. The show ran from 1951 to 1957. Today, millions of people still watch reruns of *I Love Lucy*. They still laugh when they see how funny she is. She is also remembered for her roles in the films *Stage Door* (1937) and *Mame* (1974). Lucille Ball was very talented and certainly one of the most popular actresses of her time.
>
> **(a.)** Lucille Ball
> **b.** *I Love Lucy*
> **c.** television

1. Throughout history, mustard has been a popular spice in cooking. Books from 3000 B.C. mention the use of mustard to flavor food. The ancient Egyptians, Chinese, Greeks, and Romans all used mustard . By A.D. 800, the French were using mustard to spice up their meals. It was one of the spices taken on Spanish explorations during the 1400s. Today, mustard is the most popular spice sold in the world.

    a. Egyptians
    b. spices
    c. mustard

2. Ibn Sina (known as Avicenna) was one of the most important people in the history of medicine. He was born in Iran in A.D. 980. He began practicing medicine when he was only sixteen years old. His most famous book, *Al-Qanun fi al-Tibb (The Canon of Medicine)* is one of the most important medical books ever written. It changed medical teaching throughout the world up to the early eighteenth century. Today, Ibn Sina's picture hangs in the main hall of the Faculty of Medicine at the University of Paris.

a. *The Canon of Medicine*
b. Ibn Sina
c. medicine

3. In many cities, the roads are crowded with too many cars. Too many cars can cause a serious problem called smog. Smog happens when the exhaust gases from cars mix with sunlight. Sometimes you can actually see smog. It looks like a yellow-brown cloud hanging in the air over a city. Smog spoils views and makes it unpleasant to do outdoor activities. But smog can also be dangerous to your health. It is especially dangerous for young children and older people. People with heart disease or lung problems suffer because of smog. Smog may cause headaches or dizziness, and it makes it hard for some people to breathe. Unfortunately, as more and more people drive, and the roads get more crowded, smog will only get worse.

a. smog
b. cities
c. cars

4. Powder Mountain Resort in Vermont is a great place to go for a winter vacation. In addition to the fabulous skiing and snowboarding at Powder Mountain, there are lots of other outdoor activities. You can enjoy the beautiful scenery by taking a long hike or riding a horse along the scenic trails. Or you can rent a snowmobile and spend a memorable afternoon riding in the mountains. In the evening you can go for a sleigh ride. Finally, don't forget to try ice-skating on the frozen lake.

a. Vermont
b. skiing and snowboarding
c. Powder Mountain Resort

IDENTIFYING MAIN IDEAS

Remember that a paragraph is a group of sentences about one topic. Every paragraph also has a main idea. In order to become a good reader, you also need to master the skill of recognizing the main idea of a text.

- The **main idea** is the author's most important point about the topic. The main idea answers the question, "What is the main point that the author is making about the topic?" How do you find the main idea of a paragraph?
  1. You need to read the paragraph carefully and identify the topic.
  2. You need to ask yourself, "What does the author want me to know about the topic?"

  Many times you will find the answer stated in one clear sentence. This is called the topic sentence.
- The **topic sentence** states the main idea of the paragraph, and it is often the first sentence. This is usually the case in textbook paragraphs. But the topic sentence is not always the first sentence. It can be the last sentence or even a sentence in the middle of the paragraph.

Stated Main Ideas

A. Read the following paragraphs and underline the main idea of each one. Remember that the topic sentence states the main idea.

> **Example**
>
> <u>Watching television is one of the best ways to learn English.</u> You can easily practice by listening to Americans on TV. Also, you can learn about American culture and news events by watching different programs. This will help you to understand and keep up with conversations. Your listening and conversational skills will improve a lot if you watch TV every day.

1. Gravity is the force that pulls objects toward one another. Gravity affects the largest and smallest objects. It governs the motion of all the objects in space. It keeps the moon in orbit around the earth. It keeps the earth and the other planets of the solar system in orbit around the sun. Gravity also holds you and everything else on the surface of the earth.

2. Scientists recently discovered the world's oldest playable musical instrument. It is a flute that was carved from the wing bone of a bird more than 9,000 years ago. And it is still in excellent condition. The flute is 8.6 inches long and has seven holes. It was discovered with other flutes at an ancient burial site in China. The discovery of the Chinese flutes gives people today a wonderful opportunity to hear music as it was played thousands of years ago.

3. It seems that Americans are shopping more than ever. All across the country, there are new shopping malls with a variety of stores. It's possible to buy almost anything at a mall, from shoes and clothes to furniture and electronic products. Many people also enjoy seeing a movie at the mall or eating at a food court that has different kinds of food. Most malls also have services such as post offices and cell phone stores, or even employment offices. Shopping malls have become like small cities with many kinds of stores, services, and entertainment.

4. Many beautiful flowering plants live in deserts around the world. Some of these flowering desert plants grow only when it rains. These plants have an interesting way of surviving the long dry times. Their seeds lie in the ground waiting for rain. Sometimes the seeds lie underground for years. When heavy rains come, water brings them to life. Within days, the desert bursts into beautiful color as the flowers open.

Unstated Main Ideas

Finding the main idea is not always easy. In some paragraphs the author does not state the main idea directly in a topic sentence. Then you must use all the information in the paragraph to figure out the main idea.

B. Read the following paragraphs. Use the information in each paragraph to figure out its main idea.

Example

Suzie and Harry are going to get married in July. Only their families and a few close friends will attend the wedding. The wedding will be small but very nice. Suzie and Harry are going to have the wedding outside in a beautiful park. There is a garden in the park with many kinds of flowers. They plan to take lots of photographs there. Some of their friends are musicians who play in a band, so they will provide the music. Their families will help to prepare delicious food and a big wedding cake. It will be a special day for Suzie, Harry, and their guests.

a. Suzie and Harry are planning a small wedding with the help of their friends and families.
b. Suzie and Harry don't like big weddings, so they plan to have a small one.
c. Suzie and Harry are going to get married in July.

Explanation
- Choice *a.* is correct because it best expresses the main idea of the whole paragraph.
- Choice *b.* cannot be the main idea because the paragraph never states that Suzie and Harry do not like big weddings.
- Choice *c.* cannot be the main idea because it expresses only one point in the paragraph, not its most important idea.

1. Robert has been looking at newspaper ads. He wants to move to the city, and he's trying to find a new apartment. Robert likes the excitement of life in the city. There are so many restaurants, theaters, stores, and museums. Even just taking a walk in the city is fun. The streets are filled with beautiful buildings and interesting people. Robert loves to explore different places and neighborhoods in the city. It's not easy to find a nice apartment that's not too expensive, but Robert is not going to give up looking. He hopes to move to the city as soon as possible.

   a. Robert is having trouble finding an apartment.
   b. Robert likes to walk in the city.
   c. Robert wants to move to the city for several reasons.

   (Continued on next page.)

2. Celia was so excited yesterday. She bought a new car for the first time. When she went to the car dealer, the car salesman showed her several different cars and let her test drive each one. Celia chose the perfect car with all of the features that she liked. Even the color was just what she wanted. It took more than one hour to sign all of the papers and pay for the car. Celia felt very happy when she got into her new car, and she drove all over town to show her friends. But all of a sudden, the car stopped. Celia was very upset, but then she realized what had happened. The car was out of gas. Luckily, she called a friend on her cell phone, and he brought her some gas. Then Celia continued driving her wonderful new car.

    a. Celia forgot to put enough gas in her car.
    b. Buying a new car was an exciting experience for Celia.
    c. Celia bought a new car yesterday.

3. There is an increasing number of reality shows on television. What is a reality show? In these TV programs, there are no actors. Instead, the shows are about real people. In some cases, the people are trying to win a competition. In other shows, the people are trying to change their lives by fixing up their houses or changing their style of clothing. Many of the reality shows are just about people living their daily lives as students or as a family. Some people dislike these programs, especially the ones that show too much about personal lives. However, many other TV viewers love reality shows because the characters in them are real people.

    a. Reality shows on TV about real people have become very popular.
    b. Some people love reality shows.
    c. There are no actors in reality shows.

4. The Tour de France is a cycling race that is a major event in the world of sports. In 2003, Lance Armstrong won the Tour de France for the fifth time in a row. He matched the record of Miguel Indurain for winning five times in succession. Armstrong's success as a cyclist is particularly amazing because of his medical history. In 1996, when Armstrong was the number one cyclist in the world, he found out that he had cancer. Armstrong did not lose hope. He recovered and practiced harder than ever. He went on to win many more races, including the Tour de France. Many people think of Lance Armstrong as a hero because of his hard work, persistence, and courage.

    a. The Tour de France is one of the world's biggest sporting events.
    b. Lance Armstrong won the Tour de France five times.
    c. Lance Armstrong is considered a great cyclist because of his athletic ability and personal strength.

5. On July 4, 1776, the thirteen British colonies in North America declared their independence from England. For over 200 years now, small towns and big cities all over the country have held big celebrations every July 4. It is a national holiday, so most people have the day off from work. They enjoy parades and picnics during the day and fireworks at night. Although the thirteen colonies did not win their independence from the British until 1781, July 4, 1776 is the day that lives in history.

a. The British colonies in North America won their independence in 1781.
b. July 4 is probably the most important date in the history of the United States.
c. July 4 is celebrated with parades and picnics.

More Practice Identifying Main Ideas

C. Now read the following paragraphs, and write the main idea of each one.

Example

Do you know the famous redhead Lucille Ball? She is one of the most-loved television and film actresses in American history. People all over the world can recognize her. Most people remember Lucille Ball best for her starring role in television's hit comedy called *I Love Lucy*. The show ran from 1951 to 1957. Today, millions of people still watch reruns of *I Love Lucy*. They still laugh when they see how funny she is. She is also remembered for her roles in the films *Stage Door* (1937) and *Mame* (1974). Lucille Ball was very talented and certainly one of the most popular actresses of her time.

Main Idea: Lucille Ball is one of the most-loved actresses in American history.

1. Braille is a system of writing that allows blind people to read with their fingers instead of their eyes. The Braille system was developed by Louis Braille, who became blind from an accident at age three. Louis Braille wanted to help teach blind children to read and write. Braille is not a language. It is just another way to read and write any language such as English, Spanish, or Japanese. Braille is more like a code that is based on a logical system. Every character in the Braille system is made up of one to six raised dots that you can feel with your fingertips. These characters represent the letters of the alphabet, punctuation marks, and numbers.

Main Idea: _____

2. Did you ever want to make a small room seem bigger? There are several ways to do this. Here are some tips from decorators. One way is to paint the room a light color. White, pale yellow, and beige are good choices for your paint color. Also, it's a good idea to cover the windows with simple shades since heavy fabric curtains can make a room seem small. Don't put too many pieces of furniture in the room. That will make the room look crowded and feel even smaller. One last trick is to put some large mirrors in the room to reflect light.

Main Idea: _____

(Continued on next page.)

3.   Do you collect stamps, coins, baseball cards, autographs, dolls, or anything else? If you do, you are not alone. Collecting is one of the most popular hobbies in the world. Almost anything can be collected. Even very unusual things, such as old telephones, antique toys, or insects can be collected. Some people collect things as an investment. Others collect things that they love. Some collectibles, like seashells, are easy to find. Other items are rare and require more work to find.

Main Idea: _____

4.   Most people have heard of soccer and golf. But have you ever heard of snow-snake? Snow-snake is an exciting winter game of speed and skill. Native Americans began playing it more than 500 years ago, and this traditional game is still played today in Canada. Players make a "snake" from a piece of wood about a meter long. They carve and polish the wood just like people did hundreds of years ago. The front end is shaped to look like a snake's head. The object of the game is to throw the snake down a long, narrow track of ice and snow. The person who throws the wooden snake the farthest is the winner. Some snakes go over 120 miles an hour along the icy track. No wonder people still enjoy watching snow-snake competitions.

Main Idea: _____

5.   The health club has three types of yoga classes. It is important to choose the yoga class that is right for you. If you are a beginner, there is a basic yoga class where you can learn about yoga and get an easy workout. The Ashtanga yoga class is for those who want a more physical form of yoga. It includes a lot of active exercises and helps develop balance and strength. If you want a fast class where you can practice many positions, you should take the power yoga class.

Main Idea: _____

6.   As many of us have learned the hard way, it is not fun to be stung by a bee. There are several things you can do to protect yourself from bee stings. First of all, wear light-colored clothing because bees like dark colors. Secondly, don't wear perfume or you'll find yourself a magnet for bees. If you are eating, keep your food covered. If you are drinking fruit juice or soda, look inside of the can or bottle before you take a drink. You do not want to get stung on the inside of your mouth. If bees start coming around, don't jump up and dance around. You will be safer when you don't move.

Main Idea: _____

7.   Salt, or sodium chloride (NaCl), has been a valuable mineral throughout history. In Roman times, soldiers received it as part of their pay, or salary. The mining of salt is one of the world's oldest industries. Salt deposits are found all over the world, and of course it is in the ocean. Most of the salt used for food comes from seawater. Before refrigeration, salt was an important method of preserving food to prevent it from spoiling. Salt is also used as a seasoning to make food taste better. Because salt has always been considered valuable, there are many expressions related to it. "The salt of the earth" is an expression that means someone is a good person. Similarly, "he is worth his salt" refers to someone who deserves his salary.

Main Idea: _____

> **TIP** When you read a paragraph, first identify the general topic. Ask yourself, "Who or what is the paragraph about?" Then identify the main idea. Ask yourself, "What is the author's most important point about the topic?"

Be an Active Reader

BEFORE YOU READ

A. What do you think are the ten most important inventions of all time? Write your ideas in the box, and share your list with a partner. Write your partner's list in the box, and compare your lists. Did you and your partner include any of the same inventions? Did you include any invention that your partner did not put on his or her list?

Your List	Your Partner's List
1. _____	1. _____
2. _____	2. _____
3. _____	3. _____
4. _____	4. _____
5. _____	5. _____
6. _____	6. _____
7. _____	7. _____
8. _____	8. _____
9. _____	9. _____
10. _____	10. _____

B. Read the title of the article on page 16 and look at the three pictures on pages 16 and 17. Read the captions, the words written below a picture that explain the picture. Can you guess what the article will be about? Think of three topics that might be discussed in the article.

1. _____

2. _____

3. _____

Vocabulary Preview

The words in the box are boldfaced in the article. Work with a partner and do the exercise that follows.

> **Words to Watch**
>
> | | | |
> |---|---|---|
> | accident | research | laboratory |
> | invent | melt | mold |
> | flavor | realize | microscope |

C. Match the words and phrases in the left column with the correct definitions in the right column. Write the letter of the correct definition. If you need help, read the sentence in the article where the word appears and think about how it is used.

_g_ **1.** invent

2. laboratory

3. by accident

4. microscope

5. mold

6. research (v.)

7. flavor

8. realize

9. melt

a. in a way that was not planned

b. to study something in detail

c. an instrument that makes tiny things look bigger

d. the particular taste of a food or drink

e. a special room where a scientist does tests

f. a green, blue, or black fungus that grows on old food

g. to be the first person to make something new

h. to change something from solid to liquid by heating

i. to understand the importance of something that you did not know before

Set a Purpose

You are going to read a story about several things that were invented because of an accident someone had or a mistake someone made. Look at the photographs and captions. What do you want to find out about these inventions? Write one or two questions you would like to find answers to.

Example

Who invented Popsicles and microwave ovens?

_____

_____

_____

_____

_____

AS YOU READ

As you read the article, complete the chart on the opposite page.

It Happened by Accident

1   Many inventions happen when someone is looking for a faster, easier, or better way of doing something. They are the result of years of planning and hard work. But not all of them started out like that. Lots of inventions happened because of an **accident** someone had or a mistake someone made. For example, did you know that ice cream cones, blue jeans, chocolate chip cookies, and Velcro are all the result of accidents? Some people have saved millions of lives because of an accident they had. Others have become rich by turning their accident into big business.

2   Have you ever eaten a Popsicle on a hot summer day? Popsicles were **invented** by accident by an eleven-year-old boy named Frank Epperson. In 1905, Frank accidentally left his fruit-flavored drink outside on the

"This is delicious. I wonder who invented Popsicles."

porch with a stir stick in it. During the night, it became very cold outside. Frank's drink froze with the wooden stick still in it. The next day Frank tasted the frozen drink. It was delicious. Eighteen years later, in 1923, Frank Epperson remembered his frozen drink. He decided to start a business making and selling the frozen drinks. He called them Epsicles, and he made them in seven fruit **flavors**. The name was later changed to the Popsicle.

The first Raytheon commercial microwave oven was sold in 1954. It was so large and expensive that it was used only in restaurants.

3   Many people use microwave ovens because they cook food much faster than regular ovens. But the first microwave oven wasn't invented because someone was trying to find a faster way to cook food. The idea of cooking food using microwave energy was discovered by accident. In 1946, an engineer named Dr. Percy LeBaron Spencer was **researching** microwaves. As he was working, he noticed that the chocolate candy in his pocket had **melted**. He guessed that the microwaves had caused the chocolate to melt. He decided to see what would happen if he put other kinds of food, such as popcorn and eggs, near the microwaves. He discovered that the popcorn popped and the eggs cooked. Spencer soon **realized** that microwaves cooked food very quickly. In fact, microwaves cooked foods even faster than heat. Dr. Spencer had discovered, by accident, a process that changed cooking forever. He went on to build the first microwave oven, which began a multimillion-dollar industry.

4   Penicillin has saved millions of lives since its discovery in 1928. But no one planned to discover penicillin. It happened by accident when a British doctor named Alexander Fleming was doing research on bacteria. One

day Fleming was cleaning up his **laboratory**, and he noticed that a green **mold** was growing next to the bacteria. He looked at the mold under a **microscope**. He was surprised to find that the mold had killed some of the bacteria. Fleming thought the mold might be able to kill bacteria inside our bodies that cause many diseases. He was right, and soon the mold was developed into penicillin. Fleming said, "I did not invent penicillin. Nature did that. I only discovered it by accident." Today we realize that the discovery of penicillin was one of the most important events in the history of medicine.

5   So, if you ever feel bad because you made a mistake, just remember that some of the most important inventions in the world were discovered by accident.

Alexander Fleming in his laboratory in 1928, where he first saw the penicillin mold under his microscope.

It Happened by Accident

Paragraph 2

Main Idea: _____

_____

_____

Paragraph 3

Main Idea: _____

_____

_____

Paragraph 4

Main Idea: _____

_____

_____

AFTER YOU READ

After you have read "It Happened by Accident," complete the exercises below.

Check Your Comprehension

A. True or False? Write T (True) or F (False) next to each of the following statements. If a statement is false, rewrite it to make it true.

> **Example**
>
> _F_ Accidents never turn into big businesses. *Some accidents turn into big businesses.*

___ **1.** All inventions are the result of an accident.

___ **2.** Popsicles were invented by accident by a trained scientist.

___ **3.** Popsicles were first called Epsicles.

___ **4.** Dr. Spencer wanted to find a faster way to cook food.

___ **5.** Microwave ovens were revolutionary because they cooked food much faster than regular ovens.

___ **6.** Penicillin is an important medical discovery that was discovered by accident.

___ **7.** The antibiotic penicillin has saved millions of lives.

Identify Main Ideas

B. Work in small groups. Read the following paragraphs and identify the main idea of each paragraph. Then choose the one paragraph that could be included in the article "It Happened by Accident." Discuss the reasons for your choice. Did the other groups choose the same paragraph? Compare your answers.

1. Thomas Edison (1847–1931) was one of the greatest inventors of all time. During his life, Edison designed and produced hundreds of inventions. Sometimes he worked on forty inventions at the same time! Among other things, Edison is remembered for inventing the phonograph and the motion-picture camera. But in 1879, he showed the world his most famous invention—a light bulb powered by electricity. At that time, people used gas-powered lights to light their homes, factories, and streets. These lights were dangerous and inefficient. People were happy to replace them with the new, safer electric light bulbs.

Main Idea: _____

_____

2.   Coca-Cola is one of the most popular drinks in the world. But it wasn't invented because someone was trying to find a tasty new drink. In fact, Coca-Cola didn't even start out as a soft drink. Dr. John S. Pemberton invented it in 1885 as a remedy, or medicine, for headaches. Coca-Cola tasted good, but it didn't work that well as a medicine. People eventually realized that Coca-Cola would be more successful as a soft drink than a headache remedy. So Pemberton added some other ingredients and sold it as a new soft drink. The rest is history!

Main Idea: _____

_____

3.   In 1951, a woman named Bette Nesmith Graham was working as a typist, but she was not very good at typing. She made a lot mistakes and needed to find something that would hide her mistakes. This led to her invention of a special white paint. She brushed the white paint on her papers to hide mistakes she made. Her friends and other office workers heard about her white paint and bought it from her. Ms. Graham called her product "Mistake Out." She tried to sell it to IBM. Unfortunately for IBM, they decided not to buy it. Then, Ms. Graham changed the name to "Liquid Paper" and continued to sell it on her own for 17 years. In 1971, the Gillette Company bought Liquid Paper for $47.5 million.

Main Idea: _____

_____

Work with a partner. Choose the paragraph that you think could be included in "It Happened by Accident." Discuss the reasons for your choice.

Paragraph _____ could be included in the article "It Happened by Accident"

because it _____

_____

Test Your Vocabulary

C. Choose the word that best completes each of the following sentences. Be sure to use the correct form of the word.

accident	laboratory	mold
flavor	melt	realize
invent	microscope	research

1. Don't eat that piece of bread! You should throw it away because it has _____ growing on it.

2. She is doing tests on rats in the _____.

3. I didn't spill the ink on purpose. It happened by _____.

4. The scientist is looking at blood cells under a _____.

5. Did Alexander Bell _____ the telephone?

6. He is _____ the effects of television on children.

7. Ice cream comes in many _____. My friend likes vanilla, but my favorite is chocolate.

8. The ice _____ when the sun came out. Now it will be safer for me to drive to work.

9. I'm sorry. I didn't _____ it was so late.

Sharpen Your Vocabulary Skills

USING A DICTIONARY

Dictionaries are full of information that will help you learn, understand, and use English correctly.

Guidewords

The words in a dictionary are listed in alphabetical order. To find words quickly, you should use the guidewords at the top of each dictionary page. Look at the pages below. The guideword *brotherly* in the left corner is the first word on the left page. The guideword *bug* in the right corner is the last word on the right page. Using guidewords will help you to find a word quickly.

brotherly 92		93 **bug**
broth·er·ly /ˈbrʌðə·li/ *adj* showing helpfulness, love, loyalty etc., like a brother would: *brotherly love* **brought** /brɔt/ *v* the past tense and PAST PARTICIPLE of BRING	thing: *I'll just give my hair a quick brush.* **3** [U] small bushes and trees covering an open area of land: *a brush fire* **4 a** **brush with death/the law** an occasion when	**bubble²** *v* [I] **1** to produce bubbles: *Heat the sauce until it starts to bubble.* **2** also **bubble over** to be full of a particular emotion: *The kids were bubbling over* · **bud·dy** /ˈbʌdi/ *n* **1** SPOKEN used in order to speak to a man or boy: *Hey, buddy! Leave her alone!*	*Thanks, buddy!* **2** INFORMAL a friend: *We're good buddies.* **budge** /bʌdʒ/ *v* [I,T] **1** to

A. Check the words that would be found on dictionary pages with each set of guidewords:

1. **either/element**

    ___ eldest   ___ elastic   ___ elegant   ___ effect

2. **iron/isolation**

    ___ irrelevant   ___ issue   ___ isolate   ___ irony

3. **appreciation/Arabic**

    ___ apron   ___ argument   ___ appraise   ___ approve

B. Check the words that would *not* be found on dictionary pages with these guidewords:

1. **string/strong**

    ___ struck   ___ stroll   ___ strip   ___ strike

2. **yen/yours**

    ___ yield   ___ yellow   ___ youngster   ___ youth

Meanings

Since many words in English have more than one meaning, the dictionary lists all of them. Look at the dictionary entry for *spoil*. You will see three different meanings.

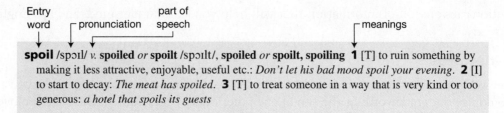

Entry word   pronunciation   part of speech   meanings

spoil /spɔɪl/ *v.* **spoiled** *or* **spoilt** /spɔɪlt/, **spoiled** *or* **spoilt, spoiling** **1** [T] to ruin something by making it less attractive, enjoyable, useful etc.: *Don't let his bad mood spoil your evening.* **2** [I] to start to decay: *The meat has spoiled.* **3** [T] to treat someone in a way that is very kind or too generous: *a hotel that spoils its guests*

Work in small groups. Use the dictionary entry for *spoil* and the dictionary definitions for the words below to look up the meanings for the underlined word in each sentence on the next page. Write the definition that best fits the meaning of the sentence.

or•gan /ˈɔrgən/ *n* **1** part of the body of an animal or plant that has a particular purpose: *the heart, liver, and other internal organs* **2** a large musical instrument like a piano, with large pipes to make the sound, or an electric instrument that makes similar sounds

di•a•mond /ˈdaɪmənd, ˈdaɪə-/ *n* [C,U] **1** a clear, very hard, valuable stone, used in jewelry and in industry: *a diamond ring* **2** a shape with four straight points that stands on one of its points –see picture at SHAPE[1] **3** a playing card with red diamond shapes on it

set•ting /ˈsɛtɪŋ/ *n* [C usually singular] **1** all the things that surround someone or something: *a cabin in a mountain setting* **2** a position of the controls on a machine, piece of electronic equipment etc.: *Turn the microwave to its highest setting.* **3** the place or time in which the events in a book or movie happen: *London is the setting for his most recent novel.*

poach /poʊtʃ/ *v* **1** [T] to cook food such as eggs or fish in slightly boiling liquid **2** [I,T] to illegally catch or shoot animals, birds, or fish, especially from private land

so•cial /ˈsoʊʃəl/ *adj* **1** relating to human society and its organization, or the quality of people's lives: *We ought to be dealing with the real **social issues** such as unemployment.* **2** relating to the position in society that you have: *friends from different **social** backgrounds* **3** relating to the things that you do with other people, especially for enjoyment: *Ellis always had an active **social life**.* **4** social animals live together in groups, rather than alone **–socially** *adv*

Example

Please put the cheese back in the refrigerator before it <u>spoils</u>.

spoil = to start to decay

1. Ever since I moved to New York, my <u>social</u> life has been great.

_____

2. Can you change the <u>settings</u> on the radio in my car?

_____

3. She won the game with an ace of <u>diamonds</u>.

_____

4. He played the <u>organ</u> for our concert.

_____

5. Mrs. Lang <u>spoils</u> her children.

_____

6. The <u>setting</u> of the movie is Toronto.

_____

7. Her husband gave her beautiful <u>diamond</u> earrings for her birthday.

_____

8. The government has increased the penalty for <u>poaching</u> animals in this area.

_____

Using Your Dictionary

Each of the following underlined words from the article has more than one meaning. Use a dictionary to find the definition that fits the word as it is used in the sentence.

1. "He was <u>right</u>, and soon the mold was developed into penicillin."

_____

2. "Others have become rich by <u>turning</u> their accident into big business."

_____

3. "Penicillin has <u>saved</u> millions of lives since its discovery in 1928."

_____

4. "He was surprised to <u>find</u> that the mold had killed some of the bacteria."

_____

5. "Dr. Spencer had discovered, by accident, a <u>process</u> that changed cooking forever."

_____

Sum It Up

Summarizing is another important reading skill. Summarizing will help you remember the important information in what you read.

Work in small groups. Imagine your friend asked you to explain the article you just read, "It Happened by Accident." First, write a list of the main points in the article. Then use the list to explain in your own words what the reading was about. Take turns explaining the article to the other members of your group.

Main Points:

1. _____

2. _____

3. _____

4. _____

Express Your Ideas

A. Discuss these questions in small groups.

1. When have you made a mistake that turned out well for you? Describe the experience. For example, you may have learned something new because you did not follow the directions when you were cooking, driving, or making something in art class.
2. Which of the inventions in the article do you think was the best? Why?
3. Do you agree that all of these inventions were important? Why or why not?
4. If you could invent something to make your life easier, what would it be?

B. Choose one of the questions above and write a paragraph about it.

_____

_____

_____

_____

_____

_____

_____

Explore the Web

A. Work with a partner. Do some research about another invention that happened by accident, such as Velcro, blue jeans, or chocolate chip cookies. Explore the Web and take notes about the invention's discovery. Try to find a picture of the invention and print it out.

 Use a search engine such as Google or Lycos. Type in a few keywords like "inventions + accidents."

B. Write a paragraph about the invention you chose. Make copies of your paragraph and hand them out to your classmates. Or, present the information about the invention to the class in an oral report. Then, with the class, discuss the inventions and decide which invention the class thinks is the most useful.

C. Work in small groups. How much do you know about inventors and inventions? Match the inventors and inventions that you know. For those that you don't know, check the Internet to find out the answer.

_h_ **1.** Alexander Graham Bell	**a.** radio
___ **2.** Guglielmo Marconi	**b.** the telegraph
___ **3.** Ruth Wakefield	**c.** polio vaccine
___ **4.** Pedro Paulet	**d.** liquid fuel motor
___ **5.** Samuel Morse	**e.** scuba gear
___ **6.** Ole Kirk Christiansen	**f.** the mechanical pencil
___ **7.** Elisha Otis	**g.** the gyroscope
___ **8.** Jonas Salk	**h.** the telephone
___ **9.** Tokuji Hayakawa	**i.** Legos
___ **10.** Jacques Cousteau	**j.** chocolate chip cookies
___ **11.** Johann Gutenberg	**k.** elevator brakes
___ **12.** Jean Foucault	**l.** printing press with movable type

Become a Better Reader

Reading well is a skill that can bring you many hours of pleasure. Good readers enjoy reading because they are confident they can read quickly and accurately. The more you read, the more confident you become and the more you will enjoy reading. Each chapter in this book has a section called *Become a Better Reader*, which will give you practice in reading for both speed and accuracy. Each of the readings in these sections contains approximately 230 words.

Do your best to read the text and answer the questions in four minutes. Then turn to page 169 to check your answers. Finally, turn to the chart on page 170 to keep track of your progress.

Alfred Lee Loomis: A Man of Science

1   During the 1920s, a very rich Wall Street banker named Alfred Lee Loomis bought a vacation house in Tuxedo Park, New York. This beautiful village was close to New York City and many rich families had summer homes there. It was in Tuxedo Park that the name of the formal suit known as the *tuxedo* originated. Men often wore tuxedos to the fancy parties they went to.

2   Loomis, however, wasn't primarily interested in socializing at parties with other successful businessmen. He was very interested in science, and he built a laboratory on his land in Tuxedo Park. It had the best equipment and became the most famous scientific lab for physics in the United States. Scientists from top universities such as Harvard and Princeton spent summers there doing research and experiments. Many famous scientists from around the world also spent time there, including Einstein, Fermi, Lawrence, and Bohr. Loomis himself became a brilliant scientist and inventor. He and his fellow scientists at the lab did important work in physics. They made key discoveries in the fields of X-ray technology, brain waves, and radar.

3   Loomis was one of the most powerful men in the United States during the period between the two world wars. He had close relationships with U.S. presidents, business executives, and the world's leading scientists. His true interest, though, was always scientific invention. He wrote, "If you want to find the truth, you must continue to experiment."

1. Alfred Lee Loomis built a laboratory in Tuxedo Park in order to
    a. have parties with other rich people
    b. wear a tuxedo
    c. do scientific experiments

2. The scientists who did research at the Loomis laboratory
    a. came only from Harvard and Princeton
    b. came from around the world
    c. came only from New York

3. At the Loomis laboratory, scientists made important discoveries in
   a. X-ray technology, brain waves, and radar
   b. the nature of the two world wars
   c. none of the above

4. Alfred Loomis was mostly interested in
   a. making money as a Wall Street banker
   b. gaining political power
   c. doing scientific experiments

Have Some Fun

A. Think about these inventions. Check the *one* invention you could *not* live without. Put a ✔ in the box.

☐ toothbrush
☐ car
☐ personal computer
☐ cell phone
☐ microwave oven

B. Now take a class survey.

1. How many students chose the toothbrush? _____

2. How many chose the car? _____

3. How many chose the personal computer? _____

4. How many chose the cell phone? _____

5. How many chose the microwave oven? _____

C. Complete this chart based on the information from your class survey.

Number of students in the class: _____ [1]

Inventions	Your Class
toothbrush	_____ %
car	_____ %
personal computer	_____ %
cell phone	_____ %
microwave oven	_____ %

[1]To find the percentage (%) of students that chose an invention, divide the number of students who chose the invention by the total number of students in the class. For example, if there are 18 students in the class and 11 of them chose the *toothbrush*, 11 divided by 18, or 61%, chose the *toothbrush*.

D. Read the following information about an actual survey. In the survey, American teenagers and adults had to choose the invention they could not live without from among the same five choices—toothbrush, car, personal computer, cell phone, and microwave oven.

The results of the survey showed that more than a third of teens (34%) and almost half of adults (42%) named the toothbrush the invention they could not live without. The automobile was a close second, getting votes from 31 percent of teens and 37 percent of adults. Of the remaining choices, teens ranked the personal computer third (16%), the cell phone fourth (10%), and the microwave last (7%). Adults rated those choices in a similar order. They named the personal computer in third place (6%). Among adults, the microwave oven (6%) and the cell phone (6%) tied for last place. (Note: Percents have been rounded to whole numbers.)

With a partner, use the information from the survey to complete the chart. Then answer the questions.

➤ Inventions	➤ Americans Surveyed	
toothbrush	Adults _____ %	Teens _____ %
car	Adults _____ %	Teens _____ %
personal computer	Adults _____ %	Teens _____ %
cell phone	Adults _____ %	Teens _____ %
microwave oven	Adults _____ %	Teens _____ %

1. Are the results of your class survey similar to the results of the national survey? _____

2. How are they similar? How are they different? _____

_____

_____

_____

CHAPTER 2

Take a Closer Look
Identifying Supporting Details

Look at the painting by Vincent van Gogh, a famous nineteenth-century Dutch painter. Discuss what you see with a partner. Then answer the questions.

1. What is the topic of the picture? In other words, what is the painting about?
   a. two chairs
   b. a house
   c. a bedroom

(Continued on next page.)

2. What objects do you see in the painting? Make a list.

<u>   *a window*   </u>

<u>   </u>

<u>   </u>

<u>   </u>

<u>   </u>

3. Compare your list with another group.

When you indentified the topic of the painting, you looked at supporting information to help you understand the painting better. In the same way, looking at the supporting information will help you understand and remember what you read.

Sharpen Your Reading Skills

IDENTIFYING SUPPORTING DETAILS

In Chapter 1 you learned that the sentences in a paragraph develop one main idea. To make the main idea clear, the author adds supporting details such as facts and examples. After you identify the topic and the main idea, you should look for details that support them. In this chapter you will practice finding supporting details in a paragraph.

Supporting details can be examples, facts, explanations, or reasons. The supporting details are not as general as the main idea. Their purpose is to give you more information about the main idea. They tell who, what, when, where, why, how, how much, or how many.

A. Add another detail to support each of these main ideas.

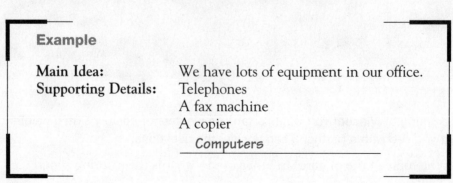

Example

Main Idea: We have lots of equipment in our office.
Supporting Details: Telephones
A fax machine
A copier
<u>*Computers*</u>

1. **Main Idea:**   There are all kinds of instruments in the music room.
   Supporting Details: A piano
                           Flutes
                           Guitars

   _____

2. **Main Idea:**   There are many ways to communicate.
   Supporting Details: Faxes
                           Telegrams
                           E-mail

   _____

3. **Main Idea:**   I love all kinds of sports.
   Supporting Details: Tennis
                           Basketball
                           Soccer

   _____

4. **Main Idea:**   There are several things to consider when choosing an apartment.
   Supporting Details: Cost
                           Location
                           Size

   _____

B. One sentence in each of the following groups is the main idea. The other two are supporting details. Write MI in front of the main idea and SD in front of the details.

> **Example**
>
> _SD_   She teaches fourth grade at an elementary school all week and works at a coffee shop on the weekends.
>
> _MI_   My sister Ellen is one of the busiest people I know.
>
> _SD_   Ellen goes to the gym after school three days a week and takes art classes the other days.

1. ____ I have very bad allergies.

   ____ I avoid nuts and chocolate because I am allergic to them.

   ____ I start sneezing if I'm around cats, feathers, and most kinds of flowers.

   (Continued on next page.)

2. ___ Mumbai, India, has a population of 18,042,000.

___ Approximately 13 million people live in Calcutta.

___ India has some of the most populated cities in the world.

3. ___ Some athletes have unusual superstitions.

___ Basketball superstar Michael Jordan always wore his blue North Carolina shorts under his Bulls uniform for good luck.

___ Soccer player Anne Morrell always sits in the same spot at each team meeting.

4. ___ The professors have flexible office hours and are easy to reach by e-mail.

___ Since I work full time, Wheeler College is the perfect school for me.

___ Wheeler offers evening programs, night classes, and online courses at an affordable price.

C. Read the following paragraphs. Identify the main idea. Then make a list of the details that support the main idea.

Example

   My trip to Miami was really disappointing. First of all, my plane was six hours late. When I finally got to my hotel, I was very disappointed. My room was small and dirty. I didn't even have a view of the beach. It started to rain on the first day and continued raining for most of the week. On the one day it didn't rain, I went to the beach, but I got a terrible sunburn. To make matters worse, my wallet was stolen, so I had to borrow money from my friends. I couldn't wait to go home. But, even the trip home was awful. The stewardess spilled coffee on my new shirt. All in all, it was a terrible vacation.

Main Idea: _My vacation to Miami was terrible._

Supporting Details: _The plane was late._

My hotel room was small and dirty.

I didn't have a view of the beach.

I got a sunburn.

My wallet was stolen.

The stewardess spilled coffee on me.

1. My cousin Jason is easy to find in a crowd. For one thing, he's really tall and towers over most people. He's over six feet tall, so he's easy to spot. Jason also has red hair that you can see from quite a distance. The best thing is that he almost always wears his favorite bright orange baseball cap. I'd recognize that hat anywhere.

Main Idea: _____

Supporting Details: _____

_____

_____

_____

2. When I got on the bus this morning, I realized that it was much quieter than usual. I sat next to a mother who was reading a book to her child. Across the aisle, a kid was looking at a comic book. A few people were busy reading the newspaper and several others were completely involved in their books. In the back of the bus two teenagers were reading magazines. I didn't want to feel left out, so I opened my backpack and took out my history textbook. Now, everyone was reading.

Main Idea: _____

Supporting Details: _____

_____

_____

_____

3. My bedroom is such a mess that it will take me hours to clean it. I haven't dusted in weeks, and there is a thick layer of dust on every piece of furniture. But before I can dust, I have to take out all the dirty dishes and coffee cups I've left everywhere. To make matters worse, I haven't hung up my clothes in days, and there are pants and shirts scattered all over the floor. I also have a pile of old newspapers next to my bed, which, needless to say, is unmade!

Main Idea: _____

Supporting Details: _____

_____

_____

_____

D. Choose one of the paragraphs above. On a separate piece of paper, draw a picture based on the paragraph. Then, think of another detail to add to the picture. Write a sentence that describes the new detail and add it to the paragraph. Share your picture and paragraph with your classmates.

E. Work with a partner. Look at the paragraphs in Chapter 1 on pages 11–12. In each paragraph, underline the details that support the main idea. Then join another pair of students and compare the sentences you underlined.

 After you identify the main idea of a paragraph, look for the details the author includes to support it. Try to find examples, facts, explanations, or reasons. Identifying the topic, main idea, and supporting details will help you understand the paragraph. Understanding the relationship between the main idea and the supporting details will improve your reading comprehension.

Test Your Skills

Read each paragraph below and answer the questions that follow. The first question is about the main idea of the paragraph. The other questions test your understanding of supporting details.

A.   The United States is a mixture of people from all over the world. The mixing started 500 years ago when European countries began sending explorers to North America. Most of America's early immigrants came from Europe, and by 1855 there were more than 3.5 million immigrants in the United States. Toward the end of the twentieth century, a new wave of immigrants entered the United States. They came mainly from Asian and Hispanic countries. Today, more than 30.5 million immigrants live in the United States, and they come from every corner of the globe. The United States is truly a nation of immigrants.

1. What is the main idea of the paragraph?
   a. European countries sent explorers to North America.
   b. Most of America's early immigrants came from Europe.
   c. The United States is truly a nation of immigrants.

2. The article does *not* mention
   a. where the immigrants are from
   b. problems immigrants face
   c. how many immigrants live in the United States

3. How many immigrants lived in the United States in 1855?
   a. At least 30.5 million
   b. More than 3.5 million
   c. Almost 35 million

B. Water is a precious natural resource, and we need to conserve it, not waste it, especially in times of drought. You can save water in your home in several ways. The first and most important thing you should do is check for leaks and fix them. A faucet that drips can waste up to 20 gallons of water every day! A leaky toilet wastes even more water. Another way you can save water is to take shorter showers. You use from 3 to 7 gallons of water every minute the shower runs. Last but not least, don't forget to turn the water off while you brush your teeth.

1. What is the main idea of the paragraph?
   a. Water is a natural resource.
   b. There are several ways to conserve water in your home.
   c. Leaky toilets waste a lot of water.

2. According to the passage, the most important way to conserve water is to
   a. brush your teeth
   b. take shorter showers
   c. check for and fix leaks

3. Which of the following is *not* mentioned as a way to conserve water?
   a. Fix leaky toilets
   b. Take baths, not showers
   c. Turn off water when you brush your teeth

C. Would you like to pay for something with camels or shells instead of paper money? Would cocoa beans fit in your wallet instead of coins? Paper money and coins have not always been the only forms of currency. In fact, all kinds of things have been used as money. In the islands of Micronesia and Melanesia, for example, feathers, cloth, teeth, stones, and shells have been used as money. In the fifteenth century, Sumatrans used human skulls. At the same time, cocoa beans were a kind of money in Mexico. Shells were popular in lots of places such as India, North America, and Africa.

1. What is the main idea of the paragraph?
   a. Many kinds of things have been used as money.
   b. Camels and shells have been used as money.
   c. Cocoa beans were a kind of money in Mexico.

2. When were cocoa beans used as money in Mexico?
   a. In the fifth century
   b. In the fourteenth century
   c. In the fifteenth century

3. Which of the following was *not* mentioned as a kind of money?
   a. Feathers
   b. Gold
   c. Shells

Be an Active Reader

BEFORE YOU READ

A. Discuss these questions in small groups.

1. A fad is something that is popular, or fashionable, for a short period of time. Did you ever buy, wear, or do something because it was a fad? For example, did you ever wear a certain kind of blue jeans because everyone else was? If so, did you lose interest in the fad quickly?
2. Are there any fads or crazes that are popular in your country now? If so, give some examples.

B. Talk to some older people, such as your parents or grandparents, and find out what fads were popular when they were younger. Make a list of the fads and share it with your classmates.

_____   _____

_____   _____

_____   _____

C. Read the title of the article on page 38 and look at the three pictures. Read the captions that go with the pictures. Can you guess what the article will be about?

1. _____
2. _____
3. _____

Vocabulary Preview

The words and idioms in the box are boldfaced in the article. Work with a partner and do the exercise that follows.

Words to Watch

fashionable	marathon	participate (in)
flagpole	contest	import
record	audience	enthusiastic

Idioms to Watch

"in"	die out	go on (went on)
"out"	take part (in)	jump on the bandwagon

D. Match the words and phrases in the left column with the correct definitions in the right column. Write the letter of the correct definition. If you need help, read the sentence in the article where the word appears and think about how it is used.

Words

_c_ 1. fashionable	**a.** a competition
___ 2. enthusiastic	**b.** a long competition
___ 3. import (v.)	**c.** popular, especially for a short time
___ 4. contest (n.)	**d.** a tall pole used for hanging flags
___ 5. audience	**e.** to take part in an activity
___ 6. marathon	**f.** showing a lot of interest and excitement
___ 7. participate in	**g.** the fastest speed, longest distance, highest level ever
___ 8. flagpole	**h.** to bring something into one country from another
___ 9. record (n.)	**i.** the people watching or listening to a concert, movie, or event

Idioms

___ 1. "in"	**a.** continued
___ 2. jump on the bandwagon	**b.** disappear completely
	c. popular
___ 3. went on	**d.** participate in
___ 4. die out	**e.** no longer popular
___ 5. take part in	**f.** start doing something because lots of other people are doing it
___ 6. "out"	

Set a Purpose

You are going to read an article about fads that were famous in the 1920s. Look at the photographs and captions. Write two questions you would like answered about fads in the 1920s.

> **Example**
>
> What was the most unusual fad of the 1920s?

1. _____

2. _____

As you read the article, complete the chart on the opposite page. Include two supporting details for each paragraph.

Unusual Fads of the 1920s

1   Did you ever hurry to a store to buy something just because it was **fashionable** and then throw it away a year or two later? You may have noticed that one year something is popular or fashionable and the next year it's completely forgotten. In other words, what's "**in**" and what's "**out**" is always changing. Something that is fashionable or "in" for a short time is called a *fad* or a *craze*. Fads have been popular throughout history, and during the 1920s, there were lots of fads. Some of the most popular fads of the 1920s were flagpole sitting, dance marathons, and mahjongg.

2   One of the most unusual fads of the 1920s was **flagpole** sitting. Flagpole sitting is sitting (or standing) on the top of a flagpole for as long as possible. The most famous flagpole sitter was a man named Alvin "Shipwreck" Kelly. One day in 1924 Kelly decided to climb up a flagpole and sit on the top for as long as he could. Although it seems strange now, flagpole sitting soon

Kelly sometimes stood upside down on flagpoles.

became a big fad. People all over the country started to copy Kelly and sit on top of flagpoles. Kelly and others traveled around the country trying to set records. Huge crowds gathered to watch flagpole sitters and cheer them on. Everyone wondered who could sit on top of a flagpole for the longest amount of time. Kelly finally set the **record** by staying on top of a flagpole in Atlantic City, New Jersey, for 49 days. During his lifetime, Kelly spent 20,613 hours on top of a pole; 210 of them were in freezing cold weather and 1,400 hours were in the rain. Flagpole sitting finally **died out** around 1929 with the coming of the Depression.

Dance marathons were a popular fad during the 1920s.

3   Dance **marathons** were also a popular fad in the United States during the 1920s. A dance marathon is a **contest** to see who can dance for the longest period of time without stopping. Young people in cities all over the country got together to **take part in** the dancing contests. One of the most famous marathon dancers was June Havoc. She began dancing when she was only two years old and danced in many marathons. The winners of dance marathons received cash prizes of up to $5,000. Dance marathons **went on** for days, weeks, and even months. Large crowds gathered to watch the dance marathons. The price to watch was less than 25 cents, and people could stay and watch as long as they wanted. Dance marathons were even broadcast on the radio to large **audiences**. The longest marathon lasted for 5,148 hours. That's almost 215 days! The contest was won by Mike Ritof and Edith Boudreaux. Can you imagine dancing nonstop for so long?

Over the years, dance marathons became more and more popular. But the dance contests could be dangerous to the dancers. In one marathon, two people died right on the dance floor. Police officers disapproved of the marathons. They often tried to stop the dance contests because they were so unsafe, especially for inexperienced dancers. The dangers, however, did not stop people from **participating in** dance marathons.

Mahjongg was played by millions of Americans in the 1920s.

4   Another fad of the 1920s was the Chinese game of mahjongg. Mahjongg is an ancient game that is played with a set of tiles. It was brought to the United States by a businessman named Joseph P. Babcock. In 1920, when Babcock was working in China, he learned how to play mahjongg. He loved the game and decided to introduce it to other Americans. He wanted to make mahjongg easier for Americans to play so he simplified the rules and put English numbers on the tiles. In the early 1920s, Babcock started to **import** mahjongg sets to the United States. The game quickly became popular and soon it was a national craze with millions of **enthusiastic** players. By 1923, more mahjongg games were sold than radios, and soon other American businessmen **jumped on the bandwagon**. Mahjongg sets were sold at prices from a few dollars to over $500. But like all other fads, the popularity of mahjongg soon died out and many stores were left with unsold games sitting on their shelves.

Unusual Fads of the 1920s

Paragraph 2

Main Idea: _____

Supporting Details: _____

_____

Paragraph 3

Main Idea: _____

Supporting Details: _____

_____

Paragraph 4

Main Idea: _____

Supporting Details: _____

_____

AFTER YOU READ

After you have read "Unusual Fads of the 1920s," complete the exercises below.

Check Your Comprehension

A. Understanding Main Ideas. Write the number of the paragraph that gives the following information.

1. Who started the flagpole-sitting craze ____

2. A popular game of the 1920s ____

3. The definition of fads ____

4. When dance marathons were popular ____

B. Understanding Supporting Details. True or False? Write T (True) or F (False) next to each of the following statements. If a statement is false, correct it to make it true.

Example

__T__ The winners of dance marathons received cash prizes of up to $5,000.

____ 1. Joseph P. Babcock invented mahjongg.

____ 2. Dance marathons were always a safe activity.

____ 3. Alvin "Shipwreck" Kelly set the record for flagpole sitting.

____ 4. Mahjongg is an old Chinese game played with a set of cards.

____ 5. Flagpole sitting died out around 1929.

____ 6. The longest marathon went on for 214 hours.

____ 7. By 1923, more mahjongg games were sold than radios.

Test Your Vocabulary

C. Choose the word or phrase that best completes each of the following sentences.

1. After the concert, everyone in the _____ stood up and clapped.

   a. flagpole   **b.** audience   **c.** marathon

2. Do you like to _____ in class discussions?

   a. participate   **b.** import   **c.** climb

3. After dancing for hours in the _____, Alice was tired and thirsty.

   a. bandwagon   **b.** audience   **c.** marathon

4. Linda always wears _____ clothes.

   a. enthusiastic   **b.** fashionable   **c.** unsafe

5. The United States _____ coffee from Brazil.

   a. participates in   **b.** imports   **c.** climbs

6. Most fads _____ after a few years.

   a. jump on the bandwagon   **b.** take part   **c.** die out

7. Mini skirts were _____ when I was a teenager. All my friends wore them.

   a. "in"   **b.** "out"   **c.** unsafe

D. One item in each list does not belong because it does not relate to the topic of the list. Cross out the item in each list that does not belong. Then, circle the topic.

Example

refrigerator   oven   ~~bed~~   microwave oven

Topic: (kitchen appliances)   living room furniture   places to eat

1. flagpole sitting   tiles   marathon dances   mahjongg

   Topic: fads   games   dances

2. mahjongg   chess   checkers   rules

   Topic: crowds   games   prizes

3. June Havoc   Mike Ritof   Joseph Babcock   Edith Boudreaux

   Topic: dancers   inventors   businessmen

4. 210 hours   25 cents   215 days   three weeks

   Topic: amounts of time   amounts of money   amounts of work

Sharpen Your Vocabulary Skills

USING A DICTIONARY

Parts of Speech

The dictionary also gives the part of speech of each entry word. The parts of speech are abbreviated as follows: *n* = noun, *v* = verb, *adj* = adjective, *adv* = adverb. As you know, one word may have many definitions, or meanings. The dictionary groups the meanings by parts of speech. Notice that there are two entries for the word <u>permit</u>. The first entry gives definitions for the verb. The second entry gives the definition for the noun.

> **per·mit¹** /pɚˈmɪt/ *v* -tted, -tting FORMAL **1** [T] to allow something to happen, especially by a rule or law: *Smoking is not permitted inside the building.* **2** [I] to make it possible for something to happen: *We'll probably go to the beach, weather permitting.* (= if the weather is good enough)

> **per·mit²** /ˈpɚmɪt/ *n* an official written statement giving you the right to do something: *You can't park here without a permit.* | *a travel/work permit*

When you come across a word that you don't know, try to figure out how it is used in the sentence. This will help you determine its part of speech. Then look at the appropriate dictionary entry for the word.

Read each sentence and determine the part of speech of the underlined word. Then look up the word in a dictionary. Write the part of speech and the correct definition on the line.

Example

Huge crowds gathered to <u>watch</u> flagpole sitters and cheer them on.
   (verb) to look at and pay attention to something or someone

1. Please put another <u>coat</u> of paint on the walls.

   _____

2. He is going to <u>nail</u> the box closed.

   _____

3. Do you have a <u>clean</u> shirt I can borrow?

_____

4. Our dog <u>guards</u> the house when we're not at home.

_____

5. My brothers love to play <u>squash</u>.

_____

6. I love the <u>design</u> on your dishes.

_____

7. Toward the end of the twentieth century, the population of the United States increased when a new <u>wave</u> of immigrants entered the country.

_____

8. He wanted to make mahjongg easier for Americans to play, so he simplified the <u>rules</u>.

_____

Sum It Up

Reread "Unusual Fads of the 1920s" and make a list of the main points. Use your list to write a one-paragraph summary of the article. The first sentence is provided. Remember to include only main ideas from the article in your summary. An effective way to do this is by answering the questions *what, where, when, who,* and *why*.

Several unusual fads were popular in the United States in the 1920s.

_____

_____

_____

_____

_____

_____

_____

Express Your Ideas

A. Discuss these questions in small groups.

1. Why do you think people take part in fads? Why do certain fads become popular?
2. What are some of the fashion fads of today? Do you like them? Why or why not?
3. What fads might become popular in the future?

B. Choose one of the questions above and write a paragraph about it.

_____

_____

_____

_____

_____

Explore the Web

A. Work with a partner. Do some research on the Web about another aspect of life in the United States during the 1920s, such as jazz, Prohibition, baseball, or the Charleston. Use a search engine and type in the keyword "1920s". Then do one of the following:

1. Draw or find a picture that expresses the topic and take notes about it. Show the picture to the class and share your information in a short oral presentation.
2. Write a paragraph about the topic you chose. Make copies of your paragraph and hand them out to your classmates. Then, with the class, discuss all the topics.

B. Look up information on the Web about these fads. Match the fads with the decade they were popular in.

_e_ 1. flagpole sitting   **a.** 1940s

___ 2. stamp collecting   **b.** 1970s

___ 3. swallowing goldfish   **c.** 1990s

___ 4. the hula hoop   **d.** 1910s

___ 5. tie dye t-shirts   **e.** 1920s

___ 6. talking to plants   **f.** 1950s

___ 7. video arcades   **g.** 1980s

___ 8. beanie babies   **h.** 1930s

___ 9. foxtrot   **i.** 1960s

The hula hoop

Become a Better Reader

Do your best to read the following text and answer the questions in four minutes. Then turn to page 169 to check your answers. Finally, turn to the chart on page 170 to keep track of your progress.

J. K. Rowling and the Harry Potter Books

1   J. K. Rowling was a divorced single mother with a baby and very little money when she first began writing the Harry Potter series. She used to sit in a café and write while her daughter was next to her taking her nap.

2   When the first Harry Potter book appeared, there wasn't much publicity for it. But within a few years, almost every child was familiar with the characters of Harry Potter and his friends Hermione, Ron, and Hagrid. Children all over the world knew all about the magic school at Hogwarts Castle where Rowling's characters learned to use magic powers and fight against the forces of evil.

3   Each book in the series has become a huge success, selling millions of copies throughout the world. Many parents, teachers, and librarians are thankful that these children's books have become so popular. Even children who don't usually like to read much outside of school love to read the Harry Potter books. Interestingly, many of the most enthusiastic Harry Potter readers are adults. Children and adults both find that these books are impossible to put down because the characters are so interesting and the story line is so exciting.

4   J. K. Rowling has said that there will be a total of seven Harry Potter books. Her millions of fans look forward to reading each one.

1. Today, J. K. Rowling is
   a. a divorced mother with very little money
   b. the well-known author of the Harry Potter books
   c. a character in the Harry Potter books

2. The Harry Potter books are about
   a. Rowling's daughter
   b. Rowling's life
   c. children at a magic school

3. Many adults think the Harry Potter books
   a. are good because they encourage children to read
   b. are impossible to read
   c. are not interesting

4. The number of Harry Potter books sold is
   a. in the millions
   b. a total of seven
   c. none of the above

Have Some Fun

Crossword puzzles were popular in the 1920s, and they are still popular today. The words in this crossword puzzle are words you have worked with in Chapter 1 and Chapter 2. Complete the puzzle using the clues provided.

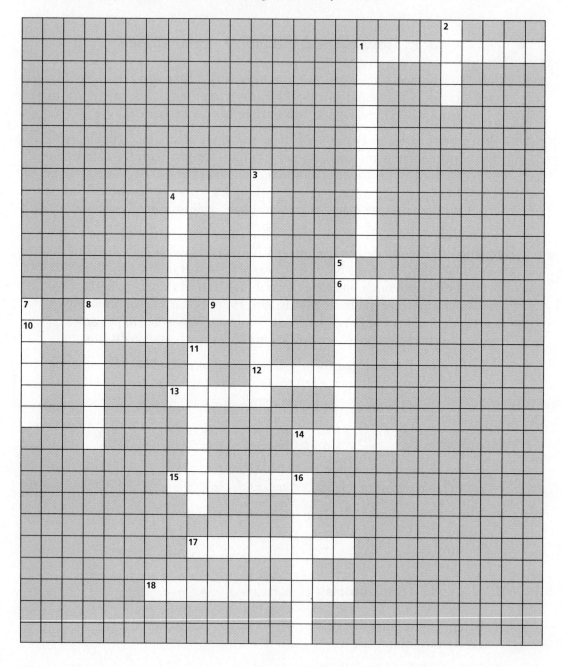

Down

1. The instrument used to make tiny things look bigger is called a
   _____.

2. The green fungus that grows on old food and other things is called a
   _____.

3. To take part in something means to _____ in it.

4. Another word for unusual is _____.

5. _____ are a popular frozen dessert in the summer.

7. The opposite of unknown is _____.

8. Many fads are popular for a while, but then people lose interest in them and
   they _____.

11. A long dance contest is called a _____.

16. When you study something in detail you _____ it.

Across

1. A _____ can cook food really quickly.

4. Alvin "Shipwreck" Kelly _____ the record for flagpole sitting.

6. If something is no longer popular, it is _____.

9. To jump on the bandwagon means to _____.

10. The group of people who watch or listen to a performance are known as the
    _____.

12. The first step to becoming a good reader is to find the _____ of the
    passage.

13. Another word for *fad* is _____.

14. The flavor of a food or drink is the _____.

15. When something is fashionable, it is _____.

17. Some of the most important inventions in the world were discovered by
    _____.

18. The words at the top of each page of a dictionary are called _____.

CHAPTER 3

Make Guesses
Previewing and Predicting

You can often guess what a movie will be about by looking at an advertising poster. Look at this poster for *The Truman Show* and discuss the questions that follow with a partner.

1. What kind of movie do you think *The Truman Show* is going to be: for example, a mystery, comedy, or documentary?

2. What predictions can you make about the movie by looking at Jim Carrey? Why do you think there is a picture of him sleeping on TV?

3. The expression *on the air* means *on TV*. What clue does "On the air. Unaware." give you about the movie?

When you looked at the poster for *The Truman Show,* you made guesses about what the movie would be about. This is called predicting.

Sharpen Your Reading Skills

PREVIEWING AND PREDICTING

Previewing and **predicting** are also skills that are important for readers to learn. Before you read something, you will often be able to *predict* what it is going to be about. How do readers make predictions? One way to make good predictions is to look for clues about the topic by looking over the whole reading first. This is called *previewing.*

Imagine that you are thinking of renting a new apartment. Before you visit the apartment, you might find out the address and the rent. Then, you might walk through it quickly to get an idea of what it looks like. You will see where each room is located, how many bedrooms and bathrooms there are, the size of the kitchen, and so on. In this way you will get an overview of the place before you look carefully at each room and all the details of the apartment. After you do these things, you will be in a position to make some predictions about whether you might be interested in renting it. In the same way, when you sit down to read something—especially a longer text like an article, book, or newspaper—you should take a few minutes to preview, or look over, the material and make some predictions about it.

Previewing means surveying a text quickly before you read it carefully. When you preview a text, look at the title and subtitles, pictures and graphics, words in bold print or italics, and introductions.

Previewing gives you an idea about what the reading is about and how it is organized. It also gives you an idea about the words that might be in the reading. The information you gain from previewing will help you make predictions about what to expect when you read. In this way, previewing and predicting are related activities.

Predicting is making an educated guess about what you are going to read. One of the goals of previewing is to help you make a prediction. You can also use what you already know about the topic to help you make predictions. Then, as you read, you can continue to make predictions about what will come next in the passage. Predicting is important because it keeps you actively involved in reading, and, therefore, helps you understand and remember more of what you read.

A. Here are some steps to follow in order to preview an article and make some predictions about its content. Use these steps to preview the article, "Lost Empires" on page 51, and make some predictions about it.

1. Look at the title of the article and write it on the line below. The title usually tells you what the article is about. What do you think this article will be about?

   _____

   _____

2. Read the subtitle. The subtitle usually summarizes the main idea of the article. Write the subtitle on the line below. What do you think the main idea of this article might be?

   _____

   _____

3. The headings that appear in colored print throughout the article give you more clues about the content of each section. Write the headings on the lines below and predict what each section will be about.

   a. _____

   _____

   _____

   b. _____

   _____

   _____

   c. _____

   _____

   _____

4. Look at the pictures in the article and read the captions that go with them. These visual aids often highlight important concepts. "Lost Empires" contains three pictures and a map. Try to guess why the author included these pictures.

5. Read the first paragraph of the article. The first paragraph is usually an introduction to the article and will tell you the purpose of the article.

6. Read the first sentence of each paragraph. This is often the topic sentence and will give you the main idea of the paragraph.

7. Now read "Lost Empires" one time all the way through. Do not stop reading to look up words in the dictionary and do not worry about parts that you do not understand. The purpose of the first reading is simply to give you a general sense of the article and to prepare you for a more careful reading.

Lost Empires

Ancient Civilizations of Central and South America

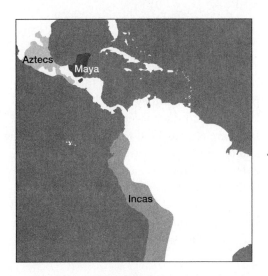

1   People lived in Central and South America long before the early European settlers established colonies on American soil. Some had built powerful empires and complex civilizations centuries before Christopher Columbus arrived in 1492.

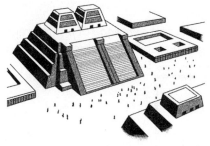

Aztec temple

The Aztecs

2   The Aztec Empire was the Native American state that ruled much of what is now Mexico from about 1428 until 1521. At the height of their power, the Aztecs controlled a large area that stretched from the Valley of Mexico in central Mexico east to the Gulf of Mexico and south to Guatemala. The Aztecs built great cities and developed a complex social, political, and religious structure. Their capital, Tenochtitlán, located where Mexico City is today, was one of the world's largest cities at that time. It had a huge temple complex, a royal palace, and many canals. By 1515, Tenochtitlán had a population of over 250,000 people.

Maya calendar

The Maya

3   The Maya civilization thrived between A.D. 250 and 900 in what is now southern Mexico and the Central American countries of Guatemala, Honduras, El Salvador, and Belize. Some of the Maya accomplishments were the development of a mathematical system that even included a special symbol to represent zero and the development of a calendar based on the orbit of the earth around the sun. This calendar had 365 days,

(Continued on next page.)

and they relied on it for planting crops. The Maya were known for their advanced knowledge of astronomy, gained through their observation of the positions of the sun, moon, stars, and planets. In addition, they had an advanced form of writing that included many symbols to represent sounds as well as ideas. The Maya kept strict records of important dates and events.

Inca road or bridge

The Incas

4   The Incas ruled one of the largest empires in the New World prior to the arrival of the Europeans. This vast empire in the Andes Mountains of South America covered over 4,000 kilometers and included parts of what is now Peru, Ecuador, Chile, Bolivia, and Argentina. The Inca Empire lasted from about A.D. 1438 until it was conquered by the Spanish in the sixteenth century. The Incas had a rich and complex civilization and ruled between 5 million and 11 million people. Although they lacked a written language and the concept of the wheel, the Incas are remembered for feats of engineering and architecture that were unequaled elsewhere in the Americas. For example, they built an extensive system of roads that covered at least 23,000 kilometers and many suspension bridges that went across the deep valleys of the Andes.

TIP   When you preview a text, look at the title and subtitles, pictures and graphics, and words in bold print or italics. Then, make some predictions about what you are going to read.

B. Read the following sentences. Each one is the first sentence of a paragraph. Use the information in the sentence to predict what the rest of the paragraph will be about.

> **Example**
>
> My new job is great.
>   **a.** Information about looking for a job
>   **b.** A description of the job
>   **c.** Reasons to get a good education

1. Buying an old used car was a big mistake.
   a. Kinds of used cars on the market
   b. Advantages of public transportation
   c. Reasons why it was a mistake to buy a used car

2. The hurricane that hit Charleston caused damage throughout the city.
   a. Information about the kind of damage the hurricane caused
   b. A history of hurricanes in the Atlantic ocean
   c. Ways to predict hurricanes

3. There are many interesting and fun things to do in New York City.
   a. A description of the architecture in New York City
   b. Examples of things to do in New York City
   c. Tourist attractions in Chicago

4. Using cell phones while driving is dangerous.
   a. An explanation of how cell phones work
   b. The advantages of cell phones
   c. Reasons you shouldn't talk on a cell phone while you are driving

C. Work in small groups. Predict what you think will happen next in each of the situations on the next page. Write your predictions on the lines. Then, join another group and compare your ideas.

Example

It's a cold, rainy night. Jane Richardson leaves Raka's Restaurant alone. She walks down Main Street and turns onto the poorly lit street where her car is parked. She looks quickly to the left and to the right. She sees something move in the shadows. She jumps.

Jane's heart starts beating very fast. She is afraid. Is someone following
her? The street is so dark, she can't see very well. Her hands are shaking
as she tries to find her car keys. All she can think of is getting in her car
safely and driving away. Then she hears a sound. Purrr. She feels something
rubbing against her leg. It's a little kitten. Jane smiles to herself. How
could she have been so frightened by such a cute little kitten?

1. Zachary is horrified when he turns on his computer and sees a blank screen. He has a paper due in an hour. The paper is written and saved, but he still needs to print it.

_____

_____

_____

_____

2. There are two seconds left in the basketball game. Matt has the ball. His team is losing by one point. Matt is the best shooter on the team, but he hurt his finger in practice this afternoon.

_____

_____

_____

_____

3. It is Susie's birthday, and she is walking home from work feeling very sorry for herself. Everything has gone wrong all day long. She had many problems at work. She is also upset because no one remembered her birthday.

_____

_____

_____

_____

4. John was feeling lucky when he bought the lottery ticket. He had just learned he got an A on the big history test, and he found the key he had lost last week.

_____

_____

_____

_____

Test Your Skills

Read the title of each of the following paragraphs and look at the picture that goes with it. Then make a prediction about what the paragraph is about. Write your prediction on the line. Finally, read each paragraph carefully and answer the four questions that follow. The first question is about the main idea of the passage. The second is a vocabulary question. The third and fourth questions test your understanding of details in the passage.

A. Claude Monet: A Master Painter of Light

Prediction: _____

Claude Monet (1840–1926) was a famous French painter and a leader in the art movement called Impressionism. Monet and other Impressionist painters wanted to paint outdoors and show the effects of sunlight. Because he was fascinated with the changing effects of sunlight, Monet often painted the same subject at different times of the day in different light. For example, he spent several months in 1890 painting a series of pictures of haystacks. He wanted to show how the effects of light on the haystacks changed during the day. After he finished the *Haystacks*, he did a series of paintings of a famous church in France. Between 1892 and 1894, he painted twenty pictures of the church at different times from sunrise to sunset.

1. What is the main idea of the paragraph?
    a. Claude Monet painted many pictures of haystacks and cathedrals.
    b. The Impressionist Claude Monet painted pictures that showed the changing effects of light.
    c. Impressionism was an important art movement in France in the late 1800s.

2. The phrase *fascinated with* in the third sentence means
    a. bored by
    b. somewhat afraid of
    c. very interested in

3. When was Monet born?
   a. In 1890
   b. After 1894
   c. In 1840

4. How many paintings did Monet do of the church?
   a. Over twenty
   b. Between 1892 and 1894
   c. Twelve

B. Keeping Your Memory in Shape

Prediction: _____

   Lots of people believe that their memory gets worse as they get older. But this doesn't have to be true for you. Research shows there are some things you can do to help keep your brain active and your memory sharp as you age. Both physical exercise and mental exercise will help your memory. Physical exercise improves circulation of the blood. This helps your brain function better. Keep your body active by walking, going to the gym, swimming, or riding your bike. Your brain, like your muscles, also needs exercise to stay in shape. Try to challenge yourself by doing mental exercises. Do crossword puzzles, read a lot, and play games that require thinking—games like chess. All of these mental exercises will help improve your memory. Remember, memory is like a muscle. The more you use it, the better it gets.

1. What is the main idea of the paragraph?
   a. Crossword puzzles are difficult.
   b. It is impossible to improve your memory.
   c. Physical and mental exercise will help your memory as you age.

2. The phrase *stay in shape* in the eighth sentence means
   a. remain the same size
   b. remain physically fit
   c. remain the same shape

3. According to the passage,
   a. games like chess require thinking
   b. reading is an example of physical exercise
   c. crossword puzzles are easy

4. Which of the following is *not* mentioned as a way to help keep your brain functioning well as you age?
   a. Eating healthy food
   b. Keeping physically active
   c. Doing mental exercises

C. A Big Piece of Land for a Small Price

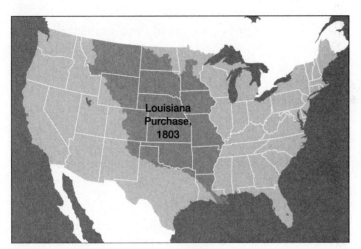

Louisiana Purchase, 1803

Prediction: _____

    In 1803, the third president of the United States, Thomas Jefferson, made a valuable purchase. He arranged to buy the Louisiana Territory from France. The size of the land was huge, and the price was cheap. The Louisiana Territory was 827,987 square miles (2,144,476 square kilometers). It stretched from the Mississippi River all the way to the Rocky Mountains. The United States paid France $15 million for the land, which was about 4 cents an acre. Many historians think the Louisiana Purchase was the greatest land bargain in U.S. history. The Louisiana Purchase doubled the size of the United States. But that was not the only benefit. It also greatly strengthened the country economically and strategically and gave the United States access to the Mississippi River. Thomas Jefferson considered the purchase one of his greatest achievements.

1. What is the main idea of the paragraph?
   a. The United States paid England $15 million for the land.
   b. The Louisiana Purchase was very beneficial to the United States.
   c. Thomas Jefferson was the third president of the United States.

2. The word *bargain* in the seventh sentence refers to the _____ of the Louisiana Purchase.
   a. size
   b. location
   c. price

3. According to the passage, Jefferson thought the Louisiana Purchase was
   a. a big mistake
   b. an expensive purchase
   c. a great personal achievement

4. Which of the following is *not* mentioned as a benefit of the Louisiana Purchase?
   a. The land contained oil and gold.
   b. The Purchase doubled the size of the country.
   c. It strengthened the United States economically and strategically.

Be an Active Reader

BEFORE YOU READ

A. Check the sentences that are true for you. Then compare your answers with a partner.

☐ **1.** I would rather watch something funny on TV than something serious.

☐ **2.** I like to tell jokes.

☐ **3.** I enjoy listening to jokes.

☐ **4.** Lots of things make me laugh.

☐ **5.** Only a few things make me laugh.

☐ **6.** I think I am a funny person.

☐ **7.** Humor is important to me.

☐ **8.** I don't like funny people.

☐ **9.** I would rather read a funny book than a serious book.

B. Preview the article on pages 60, 61, and 62. Look at the title and the illustrations. Can you guess what the article will be about? Make some predictions.

1. _____

2. _____

3. _____

Vocabulary Preview

The words in the box are boldfaced in the article. Work with a partner and do the exercise that follows.

Words to Watch

expert	humorous	burp
comedy	chuckle	embarrassed
examine	forbidden	insult

Idioms to Watch

crack up	out-of-control	frowned upon
keep a straight face		

C. Match the words and phrases in the left column with the correct definitions in the right column. Write the letter of the correct definition. If you need help, read the sentence in the article where the word or phrase appears and think about how it is used.

Words

___d___ 1. expert (n.)

_____ 2. examine

_____ 3. comedy

_____ 4. insult (n.)

_____ 5. chuckle (n.)

_____ 6. humorous

_____ 7. embarrassed

_____ 8. forbidden

_____ 9. burp (v.)

a. to look at something carefully

b. made to feel uncomfortable or ashamed, especially in front of other people

c. not allowed, especially because of an official rule

d. someone with special knowledge about a subject

e. a funny show

f. to make a noise through your mouth when gas comes up from your stomach

g. a quiet laugh

h. funny and enjoyable

i. a rude or offensive remark or action

Idioms

_____ 1. keep a straight face

_____ 2. crack up (v.)

_____ 3. out-of-control

_____ 4. frown upon

a. to laugh a lot at something

b. not possible to change, limit, or manage

c. disapprove of

d. to have a serious expression, even though you want to laugh

You are going to read an article about what makes people laugh. What do you want to learn about laughter? Write three questions that you hope the article answers.

Example

How do researchers figure out what makes people laugh?

1. _____

2. _____

3. _____

AS YOU READ

As you read the article, make predictions about what you think will come next. Write your predictions in the boxes.

Funny Business

1   Laughter is part of every human culture.

> What will this section be about?

Like language, "it's a basic part of being human," says Robert Provine, a laughter **expert** at the University of Maryland in Baltimore. Unlike language, however, laughter does not have to be learned. Babies laugh when they are as young as three months old.

2   Provine and other scientists take the study of laughter and humor seriously. "After more than 27 years of study, I can now state with certainty what kinds of things will make us laugh," says Richard Taflinger, a **comedy** expert at Washington State University in Pullman.

3   Taflinger decided to **examine** a wide range of sources, from Shakespeare to *Mad* magazine. He studied thousands of hours of television comedies. Then he identified six basic elements that can make us **crack up**. Any **humorous** situation will involve one or more of these elements, he says. If something about one of the elements is not right, a joke will fail.

4   Humanlike behavior by nonhumans is one of those elements. Can you **keep a straight face**

as you read about the other five? Look at the pictures for a **chuckle**.

5   The unexpected can be funny.

> What will this section be about?

A cow tied to a "No Parking" sign is a surprising—and amusing—image.

6   "A drawing of a dog chasing a cat won't get many giggles," says Taflinger, "but how about a mouse chasing a cat?" Now that's unexpected.

7   **Out-of-control** situations can be funny.

> What will this section be about?

In this scene from the 1950s television show *I Love Lucy,* actress Lucille Ball, on the right, and her friend are working in a candy factory. They are supposed to wrap the candy as it comes along a moving belt. But the belt is moving too fast. They can't work fast enough. As the belt speeds up, Lucy and her friend try to stuff candy into their mouths and uniforms. The more they struggle, the more we chuckle.

8   Doing something **forbidden** can be funny.

> What will this section be about?

If someone **burps** out loud, especially in a quiet library, it would be **frowned upon**. You'd probably be **embarrassed** if you did it. But your friends might laugh long and hard.

(Continued on next page.)

9   What's polite in one part of the world may be offensive, or impolite, in another, Taflinger points out. This is one reason people don't always laugh at the same behaviors.

10   Certain **insults** can be funny.

> What will this section be about?

Sometimes insults are funny but, Taflinger explains, only if you are not emotionally attached to the group being insulted. How many little brothers does it take to screw in a light bulb? Look at the answer below. "This joke's funny only to BIG brothers or sisters," says Taflinger. "Little brothers would be insulted by it." ANSWER: Three (one to hold the bulb and two to turn the ladder).

11   Silly accidents can be funny.

> What will this section be about?

When a fish bites the nose of film star Leslie Nielsen (who's only pretending to be hurt in this movie scene), people laugh.

12   "For something to be really funny, though, there must be no actual pain involved," says Taflinger. "It's humorous when someone slips on the ice and falls. People may laugh until they realize the person broke his leg. Then it's no longer funny."

AFTER YOU READ

After you have read "Funny Business," complete the following exercises.

Check Your Comprehension

A. True or False? Write T (True) or F (False) next to each of the following statements. If a statement is false, correct it to make it true.

____ **1.** Babies first laugh when they are about three or four months old.

____ **2.** Something that is polite in one country may be impolite in another.

____ **3.** Humanlike behavior by nonhumans is never funny.

____ **4.** Taflinger identified ten basic elements that make people laugh.

____ **5.** All insults are funny.

____ **6.** Laughter does not have to be learned.

B. Complete the chart with information from the article.

Elements That Make Us Laugh	Explanation or Example
1. Humanlike behavior by nonhumans	
2.	A picture of a mouse chasing a cat
3.	
4.	
5.	
6.	

Test Your Vocabulary

C. Complete the following sentences with the correct word or phrase.

burp	examine	humorous
chuckle	expert	insult
comedies	forbidden	keep a straight face
crack up	frowned upon	out-of-control
embarrassed		

1. I love to laugh. My favorite movies are all _____.

2. If you _____ these books, you will see they are all very serious.

(Continued on next page.)

3. I was very _____ when I forgot my teacher's name.

4. My father likes to tell _____ stories about his boss.

5. You shouldn't _____ your parents. It's impolite.

6. We can't smoke in this room. It's _____.

7. In the United States it is rude to _____ at the dinner table. In my family, to make that sound was _____.

8. The kids on the playground are fighting and screaming. The situation is getting _____.

9. I always _____ when I watch *I Love Lucy*. I think it's the funniest show on TV.

10. It's impossible for me to _____ when my little sister puts on makeup and tries to act grown-up.

11. Our history professor is an _____ on ancient Rome.

12. My grandfather smiled a little when I told him my favorite joke, but my brother _____.

D. Each of the following underlined words from the article has more than one meaning. Use a dictionary to find the definition that fits the word as it is used in the sentence.

Example

"If something about one of the elements is not <u>right</u>, a joke will fail."

_____*correct*_____

1. "As the belt speeds up, Lucy and her friend try to <u>stuff</u> candy into their mouths and uniforms."

_____

2. "It's humorous when someone <u>slips</u> on the ice and falls."

_____

3. "But your friends might laugh long and <u>hard</u>."

_____

4. "I can now <u>state</u> with certainty what kinds of things will make us laugh."

_____

5. "It's a basic <u>part</u> of being human."

_____

6. "People may laugh until they realize the person <u>broke</u> his leg."

_____

Sharpen Your Vocabulary Skills

WORD PARTS

Many English words are made up of several word parts called **prefixes, roots,** and **suffixes.** These parts fit together like pieces of a puzzle.

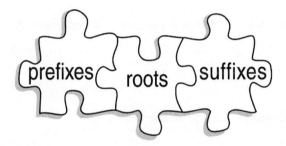

You can increase your vocabulary by learning about the structure of words and how they are formed in English. For example, the word _unfriendly_ has three parts. The main part of the word, _friend,_ is called the root. The prefix (_un_) and the suffix _-ly_ make _friend_ into the word _unfriendly._

Prefixes

One strategy you can use to figure out the meaning of an unfamiliar word is to look at its prefix.

A **prefix** is a word part that is added to the beginning of a word. A prefix changes the meaning of a word. For example, _dishonest_ means "not honest."

• My ex-husband is a **_dishonest_** man.

Negative Prefixes

Some prefixes change a word into its opposite. English has several prefixes that mean _no_ or _not._

Study the following chart to learn some common negative prefixes.

Prefix	Meaning	Example
anti-	*against*	antisocial
dis-	*not*	disobey
il-	*not*	illegal
im-	*not*	impossible
in-	*not*	incorrect
ir-	*not*	irregular
mis-	*wrongly*	misuse
non-	*not*	nonsense
un-	*not*	unable

Find the opposite of each of the following words in a dictionary. Then write a sentence for each word.

Example

legal: <u>illegal   It's illegal to park your car there.</u>

1. advantage: _____

2. rational: _____

3. regular: _____

4. approve: _____

5. literate: _____

6. predictable: _____

7. usual: _____

8. mature: _____

9. regard: _____

10. appropriate: _____

11. treat: _____

12. possible: _____

13. dress: _____

14. fat: _____

Other Prefixes

Not all prefixes change a word to its opposite, but all prefixes change the word in some way.

Study the following chart to learn some more common prefixes. Learning these prefixes will help you expand your vocabulary.

Prefix	Meaning	Example
bi-	two, twice	bilingual, biannual
ex-	no longer being or doing	ex-wife, ex–football player
multi-	many	multicultural, multicolored
post-	after, following, later	postgraduate, postwar
pre-	before	prewar, preview
re-	again, back	rewrite, redo, rewind
semi-	half, partly	semicircle, semiprecious
sub-	under, below, less important	substandard, subway, subcommittee
super-	larger, greater, more powerful	superhuman, supermarket
trans-	between two things	transatlantic, transportation

Sum It Up

Work in small groups. Imagine you are teaching somebody the information in the article you just read, "Funny Business." First, make a list of the points you want to make. Then use the list to explain in your own words what the reading was about. Take turns explaining the article to the other members of your group.

_____

_____

_____

_____

Express Your Ideas

A. Discuss these questions in small groups.

1. What kinds of things make you laugh? Are they the same or different from the kinds of things that make your parents laugh?
2. What is the funniest movie you have ever seen? What made it so funny?
3. Do you think jokes translate from one language to another? Why or why not?
4. Who is the funniest person you know? What makes that person so funny?

B. Choose one of the questions above and write a paragraph about it.

_____

_____

_____

_____

_____

_____

_____

_____

_____

_____

_____

Explore the Web

Work with a partner. Do some research on the Web about a famous comedian such as Lucille Ball, Charlie Chaplin, or Jerry Seinfeld. You may choose a comedian from the United States or any other country. Begin the search by typing in the person's name and the word "biography" as keywords. Explore two or three websites you found. Then do one of the following:

1. Find a picture of the person and take notes about his or her life. Find out why people think he or she is funny. Show the picture to the class and share your information in a short oral presentation.

2. Write a short biography about the person you chose. Make copies of your biography and hand them out to your classmates. Discuss the comedians and decide which one is the funniest.

Become a Better Reader

Do your best to read the text on the following page and answer the questions in four minutes. Then turn to page 169 to check your answers. Finally, turn to the chart on page 170 to keep track of your progress.

The CornCam Website

1   Is your idea of excitement to watch corn grow in a field? If yes, you might enjoy CornCam, a popular website at www.iowafarmer.com. CornCam shows a live recording of corn growing in a field in Iowa, a state located in the center of the United States. Visitors to the site can see changes in weather and watch the corn grow higher between spring and early fall.

2   The CornCam website also has a lot of information about corn, including a description of its uses. Corn can be used for foods such as popcorn, tortillas, and corn muffins, and it is also used to feed animals. Another recent use is as a fuel for cars and other engines. CornCam has information about farming conditions in Iowa, and there are links to many other agricultural websites.

3   Why would anyone want to sit and watch corn grow? The CornCam site has attracted millions of visitors and received more than 10,000 e-mail messages since it began in the year 2000. People love the website! They say that watching the corn grow is relaxing and makes them feel good. A lot of the messages are from people living in cities who grew up near farms, and they miss the fields and country land. Others are from people who have never seen corn plants. Many find that the view of corn growing is beautiful and comforting.

1. The CornCam website shows live pictures of
   a. Iowa farmers
   b. visitors to Iowa
   c. corn plants

2. The CornCam website has information about
   a. other agricultural websites
   b. how to fix cars and other engines
   c. a. and b.

3. Corn is useful
   a. only for food
   b. for food and fuel
   c. only for feeding animals

4. People enjoy watching the images of corn growing because
   a. they are hungry for popcorn and tortillas
   b. they like to send e-mail messages
   c. they find the pictures relaxing and comforting

Have Some Fun

JOKE QUIZ

A. A laugh a day keeps the doctor away! How funny do you think these jokes are? Match the questions with the correct answers.

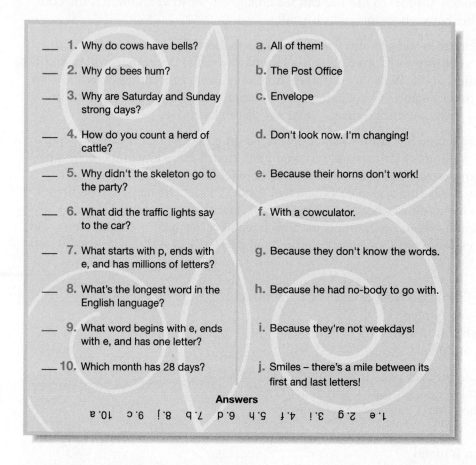

___ 1. Why do cows have bells?

___ 2. Why do bees hum?

___ 3. Why are Saturday and Sunday strong days?

___ 4. How do you count a herd of cattle?

___ 5. Why didn't the skeleton go to the party?

___ 6. What did the traffic lights say to the car?

___ 7. What starts with p, ends with e, and has millions of letters?

___ 8. What's the longest word in the English language?

___ 9. What word begins with e, ends with e, and has one letter?

___ 10. Which month has 28 days?

a. All of them!

b. The Post Office

c. Envelope

d. Don't look now. I'm changing!

e. Because their horns don't work!

f. With a cowculator.

g. Because they don't know the words.

h. Because he had no-body to go with.

i. Because they're not weekdays!

j. Smiles – there's a mile between its first and last letters!

Answers

1. e 2. g 3. i 4. f 5. h 6. d 7. b 8. j 9. c 10. a

B. Look at this sign in front of a restaurant. Do you think it's funny? Why or why not?

CHAPTER 4

Read Quickly
Skimming and Scanning

Answer the questions.

1. Look quickly at this painting by Ellis Wilson. What is the topic of the picture?

_____

(Continued on next page.)

2. Look quickly at the picture again. This time look for details.

    a. Which person is holding an umbrella?

    _____

    b. How many people are carrying flowers?

    _____

When you looked quickly at the picture just to find the topic, you skimmed it. You did not look for details, but you tried to get a general idea of what the painting was about. When you looked quickly at it to locate specific details, you scanned it. Skimming and scanning are two skills that you can use to become a better reader.

Sharpen Your Reading Skills

SKIMMING AND SCANNING

Good readers read at different speeds for different purposes. Sometimes it is important to read slowly and carefully, such as when you are reading a textbook to prepare for a test. Other times, you can read much more quickly. When you only want to find out what something is about (such as the general topic of an article), you can read it very quickly. This is called **skimming.** You can also read very quickly when you are looking for a specific piece of information in a reading. This is called **scanning.** Skimming and scanning are two important reading skills that require fast reading.

Skimming for General Ideas

 Skimming is a way to read quickly in order to discover the general idea of a text. When you skim, you do not read every word. You do not stop to look up words you do not know in a dictionary. Skimming is a good technique to use when you have lots of material to read in a short amount of time. The purpose of skimming is not to understand or remember everything you read. Instead, it is to get a general idea of what the passage is about. When you want to skim:

1. Read the first few sentences. You can often begin to get a general idea about the passage right from the start.
2. Read the last few sentences. These sentences often summarize information in the passage.
3. Look for key words (words that are repeated). They will give you clues about the topic.

Read the list of newspaper headlines. Then skim the following newspaper articles from the arts and entertainment section of a newspaper. Try to find the general topic of each article. Then match the article with the appropriate headline. Write the correct headline on the line provided.

A Night of Brazilian Music

Family Movies Are Back

Dining Mexican Style

A SAD GOODBYE

NEW ARTISTS Show Their Works

1. _____

It's a sad weekend for local music lovers. Stan's Music Shop will close its doors permanently at 6 P.M. Saturday night. Those who spent their Saturday afternoons looking through his collection of hard-to-find records, tapes, and CDs will miss the pleasures of his popular shop. Owner Stan Smith is not upset. He said that after 30 years, it was time to say good-bye. Times are different now, he said. "I loved my business, and I made a good living with it. But the music business has changed, and I'm ready for a change too."

2. _____

Maybe you have noticed that filmmakers are again making movies the whole family can enjoy. After several years of too many movies that were not appropriate for younger children and were perhaps offensive to adults, family entertainment is becoming popular again. Movies with lots of sex and violence are being replaced with drama, adventure, and human-interest stories. "A large percentage of the new movies released in the last six months are appropriate for the whole family," said The Royal Theater owner, Barbara Atkins. "We are seeing a huge increase in the number of families coming to see shows, and I think this is a good thing."

3. _____

It's not unusual for art galleries to use the summer months to invite younger and unknown artists to exhibit their works. It's an opportunity for these artists to get their work known, and it's an opportunity for buyers to see who and what is new. The Richards Gallery on South Street and the Beacon Gallery on Maple Street both have shows this month for new artists. The Richards Gallery specializes in photography but this summer it will also have several new pieces of sculpture on display. The Beacon Gallery will show oil paintings and watercolors.

4. _____

The Ari and Andreza Mendes Quintet is establishing itself as one of the most impressive music groups around. This weekend you won't have to travel far to enjoy the beat of these internationally famous Brazilian artists as they make a rare appearance as part of the Concert in the Courtyard series. Guitarist Ari has received the Sharp Award, a Brazilian award that is like the Grammy Award, for best arranger and producer. He is known for his "great music with a great heart." Critics say lead singer Andreza's voice "is so rich that he transports listeners to Brazil." This is your chance to hear wonderful music by some of Brazil's best musicians.

5. _____

It wasn't that long ago that you had to go to Mexico or at least far from this area if you wanted a good taco—one of those delicious corn tortillas that come wrapped around spicy, flavor-filled mixtures of meat, fish, herbs, and vegetables. As of yesterday, we can appreciate tacos and many other Mexican treats right here in our own backyard. If yesterday's grand opening is any sign of the quality of the food that will be offered at the Cozumel Café, we can look forward to some pretty terrific Mexican food—even when it's snowing outside. The ingredients were all as fresh as they could be, and all the dishes I tried were carefully prepared and beautifully presented. The food, the décor, and the music will make you forget you're not in Mexico—almost!

Scanning is another way to read quickly. But it is different from skimming. When you scan you read quickly in order to find specific information. To scan, you move your eyes quickly across the text. You do not have to read every word. To scan effectively you need to do several things:

1. Know the specific information you are looking for: a name, a date, a time, a key word.
2. Ignore the words and information that aren't important for your purpose.
3. Move your eyes rapidly across the text until you find the information and then stop reading.

A. Scan the following travel ad to answer the questions on the next page.

GATEWAY TRAVEL

Tour Exotic Morocco

Visit: Fez, Marrakech, Casablanca, Rabat, Tangier

9 Days / 8 Nights

Price per person: *$2,079*

Tour includes:

- Round-trip airfare from New York to Casablanca
- Round-trip airport-to-hotel transfers
- 9 nights in first-class hotels:

    Fez: Sheraton Hotel

    Marrakech: Kenzi Farah Hotel

    Casablanca: Holiday Inn Hotel

    Tangier: Intercontinental Hotel

- 8 breakfasts and 7 dinners
- Deluxe air-conditioned bus transportation between cities
- Escorted sightseeing with expert local tour guides in every city

To make your reservations call: *(800) 555-5657*

1. What is the price per person for this trip?
2. How long is the trip?
3. What is the name of the hotel in Tangier?
4. What number would you call to make reservations for this trip?
5. How would you travel between cities?

B. Scan the following listings of toll-free numbers on the Internet and write the number you would call for each of the following.

Toll-free Numbers	
Bureau of Health and Human Services	1-800-841-2900
Citizen Information Service	1-800-392-6090
Commission for the Blind	1-800-392-6450
Commission for the Deaf & Hard of Hearing	1-800-882-1155
Department of Environmental Protection	1-800-462-0444
Department of Public Safety	1-800-223-0933
Department of Revenue	1-800-392-6089
Department of Telecommunications & Energy	1-800-392-6066
Department of Veterans' Services	1-888-844-2838
Federal Aviation Administration	1-800-255-1111 (Safety Hotline)
Food Stamps	1-800-645-8333
Internal Revenue Service	1-800-829-1040
Medicare	1-800-882-1228
National Highway Traffic Safety Administration	1-800-327-4236 (Auto Safety Hotline)
Office of Consumer Affairs & Business Regulation	1-888-283-3757
O'Hare Airport	1-800-23-LOGAN
Peace Corps	1-800-424-8580
Pension Benefit Guaranty Corporation	1-800-400-7242
Registry of Motor Vehicles	1-800-858-3926
Social Security Administration	1-800-772-1213
United States Postal Service	1-800-275-8777
United States Small Business Administration	1-800-827-5722
Welfare Department	1-800-249-2007

1. O'Hare Airport _____

2. Office of Consumer Affairs & Business Regulation _____

3. Social Security Administration _____

4. United States Postal Service _____

5. Food Stamps _____

6. Federal Aviation Administration, Consumer Complaints
   _____

7. United States Small Business Administration _____

8. Registry of Motor Vehicles _____

9. Commission for the Blind _____

10. Department of Veterans Services _____

11. Department of Public Safety _____

12. Internal Revenue Service _____

C. Scan the following graph to answer these questions.

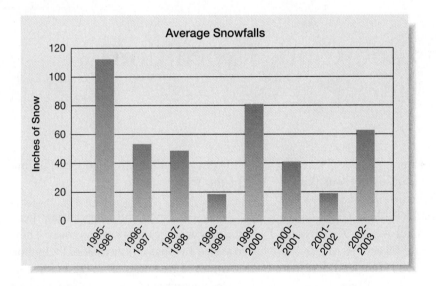

1. Which winter season had the most total snowfall?
2. Which winter season had the least total snowfall?
3. How many inches of snow fell in the 2000–2001 winter season?
4. In which two winter seasons was the total snowfall almost the same?
5. Did more snow fall in the winter season of 2001–2002 or in the winter season of 1997–1998?

D. Scan the following pages to find the specific information you need to answer these questions.

1. When did Lewis and Clark begin their expedition? _____

2. Who organized the expedition? _____

3. Where did the expedition begin? _____

4. Where did it end? _____

5. What is the name of the Native American woman who helped Lewis and Clark? _____

6. How long was their journey? _____

7. What rivers did they travel along? _____

The Lewis and Clark Expedition

1   One of the most famous journeys of exploration in American history was the Lewis and Clark expedition of 1804–06. Meriwether Lewis and William Clark led a group of explorers across the West from St. Louis to the Pacific Ocean. At that time, most Americans of European descent lived east of the Mississippi River. The West was settled by Native Americans and was mostly unexplored by the European Americans who had established the United States a few decades earlier. U.S. President Thomas Jefferson organized the expedition in order to get more information about the unknown territories and to inspire others to travel there. President Jefferson instructed Lewis and Clark to study the Native American tribes and collect information about the plant and animal life of the West.

2   In 1804, Lewis and Clark began their journey with about 40 young men. They traveled by boat and occasionally by horse along the Missouri and Columbia rivers. Later they were joined by a Native American woman named Sacajawea. She assisted the expedition by interpreting Native American languages and helping Lewis and Clark to develop friendly relations with different tribes. During most of the journey, Lewis and Clark were able to deal with the local Native Americans in a friendly manner. One of the greatest dangers they faced was grizzly bears in the northern mountains, and some of the men were injured in bear attacks. Finally, the

group reached the Pacific Ocean, then returned to St. Louis. Amazingly, during the three-year journey, only one man died, of a ruptured appendix.

3   The long trip was considered a great success, and Lewis and Clark have been admired for their courage and skill in exploring this vast, unknown territory.

Most importantly, they wrote detailed maps and journals describing the western land, peoples, plants, and animals. These journals are still of considerable interest to historians and scientists today. The discoveries of Lewis and Clark helped to increase knowledge of the western territories and led to further exploration and settlement of the United States.

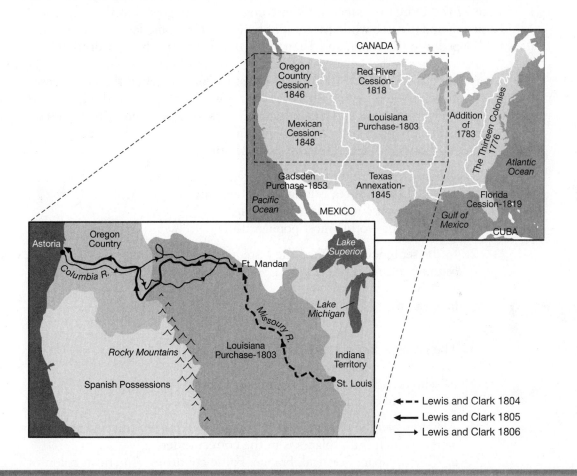

Determine your purpose for reading. Then decide if you need to read slowly and carefully, skim quickly for main ideas, or scan for specific information.

READ QUICKLY: SKIMMING AND SCANNING   **79**

Test Your Skills

Skim each paragraph below in order to get a general idea of what it is about. See if you have enough information to answer the main idea question that follows. Then go back and read each paragraph carefully in order to answer the three other questions. You may want to scan for answers to questions that ask for specific pieces of information.

A. Tea has had a long and interesting history. The story began over four and a half thousand years ago. According to legend, tea was accidentally discovered in China in 2737 B.C. by the emperor, Shen Nung. The story goes that the emperor was sitting under a tree while his servant boiled water. Some leaves from the tree dropped into the water, and Shen Nung decided to try the new drink. He liked the taste, and a new beverage was born. The custom of drinking tea spread to Japan around A.D. 600. In the 1500s, tea arrived in Portugal when the Portuguese established trade relations with China. It was then shipped to the Dutch, who in turn sent it to France and the Baltic countries. In 1650, Peter Stuyvesant brought tea to the American colonists in New Amsterdam, later called New York. Today, tea is still one of the world's most popular drinks.

1. What is the main idea of the paragraph?
   a. The history of tea is long and interesting.
   b. Tea was discovered by the Dutch.
   c. Tea is the world's most popular drink.

2. In the sentence, "He liked the taste, and a new beverage was born," the word *beverage* means
   a. baby
   b. custom
   c. drink

3. The passage does *not* mention
   a. where tea was discovered
   b. who brought tea to the American colonies
   c. the number of people who drink tea today

4. According to the passage, the custom of drinking tea traveled around the world. Which list of places is in the correct order?
   a. China, Japan, Portugal, France, Baltic countries, American colonies
   b. China, Japan, France, Portugal, Baltic countries, American colonies
   c. China, American colonies, Japan, Portugal, France, Baltic countries

B. The 1970s were a decade of fads and crazes. One of the strangest fads to hit the United States during this time was the pet rock. In 1975 an advertising executive from California named Gary Dahl created the first pet rock. He packaged the pet rocks and sold them as gifts. The rocks came in a little box with straw on the bottom. Every pet rock came with its own handbook of training instructions. Unlike real animal pets that require a lot of care, the pet rocks were easy to take care of. They were quiet, clean, and always well behaved.

In only a year, millions of people were the proud owners of pet rocks, making Dahl a millionaire.

1. What is the main idea of the paragraph?
   a. Gary Dahl was a millionaire.
   b. Pet rocks were a popular fad in the 1970s.
   c. Pet rocks came in a little box with straw on the bottom.

2. The word *decade* in the first sentence means a
   a. strange fad
   b. little rock
   c. period of ten years

3. According to the passage, real animal pets
   a. require a lot of care
   b. are quiet and clean
   c. come in small boxes

4. Which of the following is not mentioned in the paragraph?
   a. The price of a pet rock
   b. The advantages of pet rocks
   c. When pet rocks were popular

C.   The Internet is changing the travel industry. People are not making their travel plans the way they did in the past. Today, more and more people are using the Internet to make travel plans because they want to save time and money. They think they can find the best prices for plane tickets, hotel reservations, and car rentals on the internet. They are looking for online discounts and last-minute deals for their travel plans. Travel is the biggest category of online purchases by U.S. consumers. Studies show that 64 million Americans now research their travel choices online. This is a big jump from 1997, when just 12 million Americans used the Internet to make travel plans.

1. What is the main idea of the paragraph?
   a. Many people use the Internet to make hotel reservations.
   b. The Internet is changing the travel industry.
   c. People buy many kinds of things on the Internet.

2. The word *category* in the sixth sentence means
   a. group
   b. price
   c. ticket

3. In 1997, how many Americans used the Internet to make travel plans?
   a. 59 million
   b. 12 million
   c. 64 million

4. The paragraph does not mention
   a. how people made their travel plans in the past
   b. why people use the Internet to make travel plans
   c. how many Americans use the Internet to make travel plans

Be an Active Reader

BEFORE YOU READ

A. Discuss these questions with a partner.

1. How do you stay warm when it's cold outside?
2. Have you ever seen a polar bear in a zoo or on TV?
3. Do you know how polar bears stay warm?

B. Preview and predict. Read the title and subtitle of the article on pages 84 and 85. Read the headings in color. Look at the map and photograph. Can you guess what the article will be about? Think of three topics that might be discussed in the article.

1. _____
2. _____
3. _____

C. Skim the article to find the number of the paragraph that answers each question.

1. How do polar bears keep warm in the cold Arctic environment? ___
2. What do pregnant females do in the winter? ___
3. How do polar bears avoid overheating? ___
4. How do polar bears move on ice and swim in icy water? ___

Vocabulary Preview

The words in the box are boldfaced in the article. Work with a partner and do the exercise that follows.

> **Words to Watch**
>
> | island | adapted | biologist |
> |--------|---------|-----------|
> | coast | hollow | sharp |
> | frigid | avoid | species |
>
> **Idioms to Watch**
>
> | cope with | curl up | got it covered |
> |-----------|---------|----------------|
> | no sweat | | |

D. Match the words and phrases in the left column with the correct definitions in the right column. Write the letter of the correct definition. If you need help, read the sentence in the article where the word appears and think about how it is used.

Words

___f___ **1.** frigid   **a.** a piece of land completely surrounded by water

_____ **2.** hollow   **b.** the land next to an ocean

_____ **3.** coast (n.)   **c.** a group of animals or plants of the same kind

_____ **4.** island   **d.** having an empty space inside

_____ **5.** adapted (adj.)   **e.** a scientist who studies living things

_____ **6.** avoid   **f.** very cold

_____ **7.** sharp   **g.** to try not to do something

_____ **8.** biologist   **h.** changed to suit the environment

_____ **9.** species   **i.** having an edge or point that can cut things easily

Idioms

_____ **1.** cope with   **a.** no problem

_____ **2.** curl up   **b.** in control of a situation

_____ **3.** got it covered   **c.** to succeed in dealing with a difficult problem

_____ **4.** no sweat   **d.** to lie with your arms and legs bent close to your body

Set a Purpose

You are going to read an article about polar bears. Write two or three questions you would like answered about polar bears.

> **Example**
>
> How do polar bears keep warm? _____

1. _____

2. _____

3. _____

Bear Necessities
How Polar Bears Survive the Deep Freeze

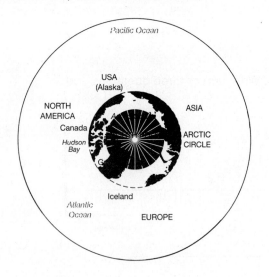

1   Polar bears are found all around the North Pole on sea ice, **islands**, and **coasts**. In the polar bears' **frigid** Arctic home, winter temperatures can fall as low as –45°C. Luckily, polar bears are perfectly **adapted** to live in their frozen, harsh environment.

Keeping Warm

2   So, what keeps the polar bears so toasty in the Arctic deep freeze? Their best protection from the cold is their thick, white fur coat that keeps them warm even on the coldest days. The fur coat has two layers. There is a thick, soft underlayer of fur next to their skin and an outer layer of long, thinner hairs called *guard hairs*. The guard hairs are **hollow** tubes like drinking straws that direct the sun's rays to the bear's skin. A polar bear looks white, but under its fur the skin is black. Dark skin can absorb more heat than light skin, so it helps keep the polar bear warm. Another way a polar bear **copes with** the cold is with built-in insulation. Polar bears have a layer of blubber, or fat, under their skin that can be more than four inches thick. Like other kinds of insulation, blubber stops heat from getting out. The bear's thick fur, dark skin, and fat keep it warm in icy water as well as on land.

Cooling Off

3   Keeping warm is **no sweat** for a polar bear—in fact, sometimes its biggest problem is cooling off! Imagine running around outside in a winter coat. Even if it's cold out, you might start to feel too warm. And like you in that coat, a polar bear is so well insulated that it can easily become overheated, or too hot, by moving too fast. But, polar bears know how to **avoid** overheating. For one thing, a polar bear usually moves slowly and doesn't run very often. In addition, "It will often grab a mouthful of snow to cool off," says polar bear **biologist** François Messier. "Or it may lie flat with its legs extended to expose its

stomach directly to the snow, since belly fur isn't as thick."

Moving Around on Ice

4   Polar bears are also well adapted to move around on ice. A polar bear spends the winter living on sea ice—ice formed when the ocean freezes. But the bear has no trouble keeping its footing on slippery ground. Its paws are perfect for getting around on a slick, cold surface. They have rough pads to keep them from slipping on the ice. The thick fur between the pads keeps the bear's feet warm. It uses the **sharp**, curved claws on its front paws like hooks to climb onto the ice from the water. Polar bears' claws also help them dig in the ice when they hunt for seals to eat.

Getting Out of the Cold

5   Finally, some polar bears—pregnant females—have adapted to the cold by hibernating (sleeping in the winter.) They dig a den in the fall, give birth inside in early winter, and stay there until spring. With a big, warm polar bear inside it, the den's temperature can be 40 degrees higher than the outside. Although male polar bears don't hibernate, there are stormy times when wind and blowing snow make travel and hunting too difficult. "So they just **curl up** and let the snow cover them," says Messier. "It's warmer under the snow than it is being exposed to the air."

6   "People tend to view the Arctic as a harsh environment," says Messier. "But if you have a **species** with the correct adaptations, then it's not necessarily a harsh environment for them." So bring on the snow, wind, and icy water. Because when it comes to keeping warm, a polar bear's **got it covered**!

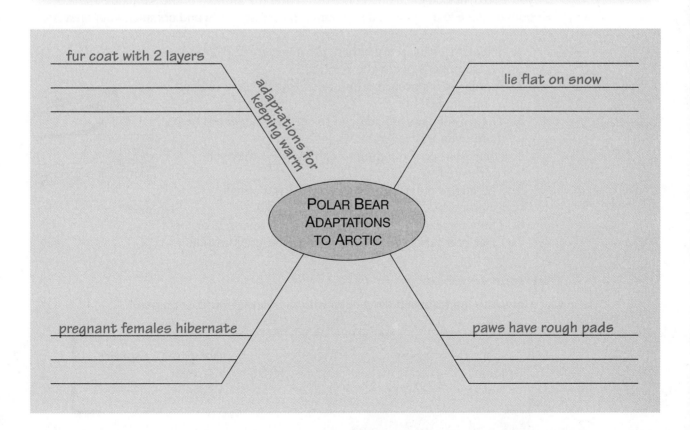

AFTER YOU READ

After you have read "Bear Necessities," complete the following exercises.

Check Your Comprehension

A. True or False? Write T (True) or F (False) next to each of the following statements. If a statement is false, correct it to make it true.

_____ **1.** A polar bear's coat is made up of two layers.

_____ **2.** A polar bear's skin is white.

_____ **3.** All polar bears hibernate in the winter.

_____ **4.** Female polar bears give birth in a den.

_____ **5.** Polar bears have thin guard hairs.

_____ **6.** Polar bears usually run quickly from place to place.

_____ **7.** Polar bears use their claws to hunt seals.

_____ **8.** The fur on a polar bear's belly is thinner than the fur on its back.

Add More Details

B. Work with a partner. Read the following list of facts about polar bears. Decide which ones you would use as details in the article "Bear Necessities." Then figure out where you would include each one in the text. Write the number of the sentence in the correct place in the article. Join another pair of students and compare your answers.

1. Scientists estimate that there are between 22,000 and 27,000 polar bears in the Arctic.
2. A polar bear's nose and lips, as well as the skin under its fur, are black.
3. Their hind paws are adapted to act like rudders to help them swim in the Arctic waters.
4. Polar bears go swimming to cool down if they get overheated.
5. The largest polar bear ever recorded was a male weighing 1,002 kilograms (2,209 pounds).
6. Their compact ears and small tail also prevent heat loss.
7. Polar bear fur is waterproof, making it a great insulator.

a rudder

Test Your Vocabulary

C. Complete the following sentences with the correct word or phrase.

adapted	coast	frigid	island	species
avoid	cope with	got it covered	no sweat	
biologist	curl up	hollow	sharp	

1. You can drink water through a straw because it is _____.

2. Would you like to live in a harsh, _____ climate?

3. Be careful! That knife is very _____.

4. Polar bears are well _____ to their environment.

5. My son likes to _____ on the couch and watch TV.

6. Sure, I can finish this job before noon: _____!

7. How will you _____ all the responsibility?

8. The situation at work isn't that bad. I've _____.

9. I love the beaches on the Pacific _____.

10. You should bring an umbrella if you want to _____ getting wet.

11. There is a wonderful hotel on this _____.

12. Dr. Davis is a _____ who studies the plants and animals of Costa Rica.

13. There are many unusual _____ of animals in Australia.

D. One word in each of the following lists does not belong. Cross out that word. Then, find a partner and explain your decision.

Example

| run | swim | ~~winter~~ | dig |

1. nap — hunt — hibernate — sleep
2. September — winter — spring — summer
3. paws — ears — stomach — seal
4. icy — cold — toasty — frigid
5. hair — fur — skin — den
6. running — claws — swimming — hunting
7. toasty — jacket — warm — hot
8. land — sea — blubber — island
9. polar — cold — arctic — common
10. fur — jacket — blubber — wind
11. white — black — sky — blue
12. sleet — snow — measure — rain

Sharpen Your Vocabulary Skills

Synonyms and Antonyms

One way to expand your vocabulary and help you remember new words is by learning synonyms and antonyms.

- A **synonym** is a word that has the same meaning as another word.
  For example, *sad* is a synonym of *unhappy*.
- An **antonym** is a word that has the opposite meaning of another word.
  For example, *sad* is an antonym of *happy*.

Learning synonyms and antonyms of new words will increase your vocabulary.

Write an S if the words are synonyms. Write an A if the words are antonyms. Use your dictionary to look up the meanings of unfamiliar words.

Example

| thick | thin | A |

1. contest	competition	___
2. fashionable	unpopular	___
3. ancient	current	___
4. dozen	twelve	___
5. advice	guidance	___
6. journalist	reporter	___
7. accident	mistake	___
8. invent	create	___
9. foolish	wise	___
10. criticize	praise	___
11. stomach	belly	___
12. harsh	severe	___
13. toasty	chilly	___
14. dense	thick	___
15. absorb	reflect	___
16. cope with	manage	___

Sum It Up

Work with a partner. Reread "Bear Necessities," and write a one-paragraph summary of the article. Then, join another pair and compare the summaries. What points did you both include?

_____

_____

_____

_____

Express Your Ideas

A. Discuss these questions in small groups.

1. Have you ever visited a place with a very cold climate? What was it like?
2. What other animals do you know of that have adapted to very cold climates? What about very dry climates or very hot climates?
3. What are some of the ways that humans have adapted to harsh environments?

B. Choose one of the questions above and write a paragraph about it.

_____

_____

_____

_____

Explore the Web

Work with a partner. Adaptations are the special characteristics that enable animals to survive in their environment. Use the Internet to do some research about how another animal has adapted to life in a harsh environment. For example, find out how camels or lizards have adapted to the desert or how emperor penguins or seals survive in the Antarctic. Then do one of the following:

1. Draw or find a picture of the animal and take notes about how it lives. How does it adapt to life in a harsh environment? Show the picture to the class and share your information in a short oral presentation.

2. Write a paragraph about the animal you chose. Make copies of your paragraphs and hand them out to your classmates.

Become a Better Reader

Do your best to read the following text and answer the questions in four minutes. Then turn to page 169 to check your answers. Finally, turn to the chart on page 170 to keep track of your progress.

The Great Wall of China

1   One of the great wonders of the world is the Great Wall of China. This amazing architectural structure runs about 4,500 miles (7,300 km) across China from east to west. It was built over many centuries, and the work was all done by hand.

2   The Great Wall has guard towers all along its length. In most sections, the wall is about 30 feet (9 m) high and the guard towers are about 40 feet (12 m) high. The purpose of the towers was to have a place for guards to watch out for enemy soldiers who might be trying to attack China. Another purpose was to provide communication along the wall. At night fires were used, and during the day smoke was used as a signal. In this way, towns across China could send messages along the wall to the capital.

3   Parts of the Great Wall were built as early as the seventh century B.C. Major construction of the wall took place in 214 B.C. The emperor of China, Shih Huangdi, ordered more construction around 210 B.C. to connect all of the different parts of the wall throughout China. In later centuries, there was more building and repair of the wall. Today parts of the Great Wall have fallen down and no longer exist. The remaining sections of the wall are still very impressive, and the Great Wall is a major tourist attraction.

1. Construction of the Great Wall of China
   a. began in the last century
   b. occurred over a period of many centuries
   c. was finished in 214 B.C.

2. The guard towers were built
   a. as a place to look out for enemy soldiers
   b. as a method of communication across China
   c. a. and b.

3. Shih Huangdi was
   a. a Chinese emperor
   b. the architect of the Great Wall
   c. an enemy soldier

4. The Great Wall
   a. no longer exists
   b. has been completely repaired
   c. still exists, but some sections are missing

Have Some Fun

ARTIC ADAPTATION QUIZ

How much do you know about animals that live in the Arctic?
Take this quiz to find out. Look at the pictures and match each animal with its description.

1. Which Arctic animal is an herbivore with antlers? It has thick brown fur that traps air and insulates it from the cold and helps it float in water. _____

2. Which animal has short ears, very big, strong back legs, and huge back feet to leap on the snow? _____

3. Which animal's fur is gray-brown in the summer and white during the winter, making it hard to see in the snow? _____

4. Which animal lays its eggs in the Arctic snow? _____

5. Which seal-eating animal has two types of fur to keep it warm? _____

6. Which animal has a red and yellow beak to store food, orange webbed feet to help it swim, and thick, waterproof feathers that protect it from the cold? _____

7. Who has a huge body with very long fur, a big hump on its shoulders, and hoofed feet? _____

8. Whose thickset body is covered with black skin with white patches? It has one tall fin and large flippers that look like paddles. _____

9. What small, furry animal has a tiny face, sharp teeth and claws, and a tail with black fur at the tip? _____

10. Which large, noisy mammal spends most of its life in the sea, but likes to sunbathe on the beach, too? It has reddish-brown fur and grows two tusks. _____

arctic fox

arctic hare

ermine

walrus

puffin

reindeer

snow goose

musk ox

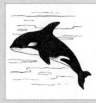
killer whale

polar bear

Answers

1. reindeer
2. arctic hare
3. arctic fox
4. snow goose
5. polar bear
6. puffin
7. musk ox
8. killer whale
9. ermine
10. walrus

CHAPTER 5

Figure It Out
Using Context Clues

"Class, I've got a lot of material to cover, so to save time I won't be using vowels today. Nw lts bgn, pls trn t pg 122."

Look at the cartoon and discuss it with a partner. Then answer the questions.

1. Do you think the cartoon is funny? Why or why not?

_____

2. What do you think "Nw lts bgn, pls trn t pg 122" means?

_____

3. What clues did you use to figure out the meaning?

_____

Sharpen Your Reading Skills

USING CONTEXT CLUES TO GUESS MEANING

The English language has more words than any other language—over a million of them—and many have several meanings. Obviously, it is impossible to memorize the meanings of all these words. The good news is that you don't need to. Like all good readers, you can develop strategies and use **clues** (information that helps you solve a problem) to help you figure out the meanings of words you don't know. Often it is not necessary to know the exact meaning of a certain word to understand the sentence in which it occurs.

One strategy you can use to figure out the meaning of an unfamiliar word is to use the **context** (the words and sentences around the word) to guess the meaning. In this chapter, you will learn four kinds of **context clues**: definition clues, comparison clues, contrast clues, and example clues.

Definition Clues

Sometimes a word that you don't know is **defined or explained** right in the sentence. The underlined words in the following sentences are all defined in the same or next sentence. The definitions are circled.

- A vertebrate is an animal with a backbone.
- Proverbs are old but familiar sayings that usually give advice.
- The time of year when day and night are equal in length everywhere is known as an equinox.
- The study of the origin or words is called etymology.
- A tsunami, or huge ocean wave, can be very dangerous.

The meaning of a word is sometimes in **parentheses**, between **commas**, or after a **dash**. Here are some examples:
- The three main groups of dinosaurs are herbivores (animals that eat plants), carnivores (animals that eat other animals), and omnivores (animals that eat plants and other animals).
- The surgeon x-rayed my femur, leg bone, to see if it was broken.
- After taking a course in paleontology—the study of fossils—Pam decided to change her major.

A. Use definition clues to write a definition for the underlined word in each of the following sentences. Do not use your dictionary.

> **Example**
>
> A period of one thousand years is known as a <u>millennium</u>.
>
>   _A millennium is a period of one thousand years._

1. The lawyer wants to change the <u>venue</u> (place where an event is held) of his client's trial.

   _____

2. <u>Zoologists</u>, people who study animals, are particularly interested in dragonflies, but everyone can enjoy their colors and shapes.

   _____

3. Starfish are very <u>scarce</u>—rare—in this part of the world.

   _____

4. Trees that lose their leaves every year are called <u>deciduous trees</u>.

   _____

5. The doctor said the patient has <u>hypertension</u>, also known as high blood pressure.

   _____

6. When you are <u>perplexed</u> about something, you are confused.

   _____

7. The idiom _<u>in hot water</u>_ means in trouble.

   _____

8. He majored in <u>archaeology</u>, the study of prehistoric cultures.

   _____

9. Mathematicians use a tool called a <u>protractor</u> to measure angles.

   _____

10. Her solution to the problem was <u>pragmatic</u> (sensible and practical).

   _____

11. Childhood <u>obesity</u>, or fatness, is a growing problem.

   _____

Comparison Clues

Sometimes you can figure out the meaning of a word because the sentence contains a word such as *also* or *like* that indicates a **comparison** between two **similar ideas**. Look at the following example.

- Jason was <u>astounded</u> when he won first prize, and I was also surprised.

The word *also* gives you the clue that *astounded* means the same as *surprised*.

Other words or phrases that indicate a comparison between two similar ideas: *as, just as, too, and, similarly, similar to, related, resembling*.

B. Use comparison clues to write a definition of the underlined word in each of the following sentences. Do not use your dictionary.

Example

John said he was <u>furious</u> when he read the note. I was also very angry after he showed it to me.

Furious means very angry.

1. Like my father's <u>commands</u>, my mother's orders seem reasonable.

   _____

2. Water and fuel are both precious natural resources. Just as we need to <u>conserve</u> fuel, we need to save water, especially in times of drought. There are several easy ways to save water in your home.

   _____

3. This article will give you some <u>tips</u> to help keep your pet cool in the summer heat. Your veterinarian can give you some suggestions too. The first suggestion is to give your pet lots of water throughout the day.

   _____

4. The whole team was <u>let down</u> when we lost the game, and the coach was just as disappointed.

   _____

5. I'm <u>terrified</u> of snakes. Similarly, I'm scared of spiders.

   _____

Contrast Clues

Sometimes you can figure out the meaning of a word because the sentence contains a word such as *but* or *however* that indicates a **contrast** between two **opposite ideas**. Look at the example.

- My jeans are <u>filthy</u>, but my T-shirt is clean.

The word *but* gives you the clue that *filthy* means the opposite of *clean*.

Other words or phrases that indicate a contrast between two opposite ideas: ***not, on the other hand, unlike, instead, even though, although, in contrast.***

C. Use contrast clues to write a definition of the underlined word in each of the following sentences. Do not use your dictionary.

> **Example**
>
> Although my cat is usually <u>lethargic</u> on hot days, he has lots of energy today.
>
> *Lethargic means having very little energy.*

1. The temperature here <u>varies</u> a lot. In contrast, the temperature in my hometown usually stays the same.

   _____

2. Lisa is a <u>diligent</u> student, but her sister doesn't work hard in school.

   _____

3. My father wants to <u>retire</u> when he turns 65. On the other hand, my mother plans to keep working.

   _____

4. When you told me the story, it sounded <u>incredible</u>. But now that I've read more about it, the story seems believable.

   _____

5. We need to <u>conserve</u> water, not waste it, especially in times of drought.

   _____

6. One of my roommates is <u>loquacious</u>, but the other one rarely talks at all.

   _____

7. I usually like to plan everything down to the smallest detail. However, I try to be more <u>spontaneous</u> when I go on vacation.

   _____

Example Clues

Sometimes a writer gives an **example** or examples to help explain an unfamiliar word. The example(s) will help you figure out the general meaning of the word if it is new to you. Expressions like **such as, for instance, for example,** and **like** introduce example clues. Look at these examples.

- <u>Fast food</u>, such as hamburgers, French fries, and pizza, is often a big part of a teenager's diet.

You might not know the exact definition of *fast food*, but from the examples in the sentence you can guess that it means something like *inexpensive and quickly served food.*

- Pam is a <u>versatile</u> singer. For example, she can sing jazz, rock 'n' roll, and even opera.

Using the examples in the sentence, you can figure out that *versatile* means *good at doing a lot of different things.*

D. Use example clues to write a general definition of the underlined word in each of the following sentences. Do not use your dictionary.

> **Example**
>
> English has lots of <u>homophones</u>, such as two/too and bear/bare.
>
> *Homophones are words that sound alike but are spelled differently.*

1. Jessie is an <u>indulgent</u> mother. For instance, she lets her daughter eat as much candy as she wants, stay up late, and miss school.

   _____

2. <u>White-collar workers</u>, such as doctors, lawyers, professors, and bankers, usually work in offices. <u>Blue-collar workers</u> like construction workers, mechanics, and truck drivers often work in factories, farms, or mines.

   _____

   _____

3. Alan is a very <u>frugal</u> person. For example, he always uses store coupons, and he rarely goes to restaurants, preferring to save money by cooking at home.

   _____

4. Ever since I was a child, I have liked to play percussion instruments like <u>drums</u>.

   _____

5. Most <u>apes</u>, such as gorillas and chimpanzees, are very social animals.

   _____

E. Put It Together. Read these sentences from the article "Bear Necessities" in Chapter 4. Use any vocabulary-in-context clues to write a general definition of the underlined word in each of the following sentences.

Example

A polar bear is so well insulated that it can easily become <u>overheated</u>, or too hot, by moving too fast.

Overheated means too hot.

1. What keeps the polar bears so <u>toasty</u> in the Arctic deep freeze? Their best protection from the cold is their thick, white fur coat that keeps them warm even on the coldest days.

_____

2. Or it may lie flat with its legs extended to expose its stomach directly to the snow, since <u>belly</u> fur isn't as thick.

_____

3. A polar bear spends the winter living on <u>sea ice</u>—ice formed when the ocean freezes.

_____

4. It uses the sharp, curved <u>claws</u> on its front paws like hooks to climb onto the ice from the water.

_____

5. Finally, some polar bears—pregnant females—have adapted to the cold by <u>hibernating</u> (sleeping in the winter).

_____

6. Polar bears have a layer of <u>blubber</u>, or fat, under their skin that can be more than four inches thick.

_____

7. Like other kinds of <u>insulation</u>, blubber stops heat from getting out.

_____

 It is not always necessary to stop reading and look up a new word in the dictionary for an exact definition. First try to use clues in the sentence to help you figure out the meaning. Learn to be satisfied with the general meaning of a word.

Test Your Skills

Read each paragraph below and answer the questions. The first question is about the topic or the main idea. The second is a vocabulary question. The third and fourth questions test your understanding of details in the passage.

A.   People have used wind power as a natural source of energy for many centuries. Over 5,000 years ago, the ancient Egyptians used the wind to sail ships on the Nile River. In the seventh century, the Persians built windmills to grind wheat and other grains. By the twelfth century, the use of windmills had spread to Europe, where they were also used for pumping water. During the 1800s, windmills traveled to other parts of the world and were used to produce electricity. Recently, there has been renewed interest in using wind power to produce electricity. In fact, nowadays wind power is the fastest-growing renewable energy source in the world. Wind power's showplace is Denmark, where 18 percent of the energy supply comes from wind.

1. What is the topic of the paragraph?
   a. Wind power
   b. Denmark
   c. Energy sources

2. What does the word *spread* in the fourth sentence mean?
   a. Folded
   b. Traveled
   c. Decreased

3. When did windmills arrive in Europe?
   a. In the seventh century
   b. In the 1800s
   c. By the twelfth century

4. Which idea is not mentioned in the paragraph?
   a. Wind power is more important than solar power.
   b. Wind power has been used to grind grain, pump water, and produce energy.
   c. Wind power is the fastest-growing renewable energy source in the world.

B.   Sometimes when plants and animals die, parts of their bodies are preserved in rocks. These are called *fossils*. A fossil may be a tooth, a bone, a leaf, a seed, or anything that is hard. Fossils are as old as the rocks they are found in. Some were formed millions of years ago. Fossils are important to our understanding of the earth's history. Fossils are valuable because scientists can learn a lot by studying them. They can use the fossils to form a picture of what life was like millions of years ago. They tell scientists which plants and animals lived in prehistoric times and where they lived. They also tell something about when they lived. Depending on the position of fossils in the layers of the earth's crust, scientists can figure out which animals lived before other animals and which animals lived at the same time.

1. What is the main idea of the paragraph?
   a. Most fossils have been formed recently.
   b. Fossils can teach us a lot about life in the past.
   c. A fossil can be a bone or a tooth.

2. What does the word *position* mean in the last sentence?
   a. Size
   b. Opinion
   c. Place

3. According to the passage, which statement is not true about fossils?
   a. They are older than the rocks they are found in.
   b. They are important to our understanding of the earth's history.
   c. Some were formed millions of years ago.

4. Fossils can be
   a. teeth and bones
   b. seeds and leaves
   c. all of the above

C.   Mohandas Gandhi was one of the most influential leaders of the twentieth century. Many people call Gandhi the father of India because of his leadership in India's fight for independence from British rule. Gandhi believed in resisting injustice in a peaceful, nonviolent way. This is called "passive resistance." Few leaders have done more for peace than Gandhi. Gandhi influenced the thinking of many other leaders around the world. For example, the American civil rights leader Martin Luther King, Jr., was inspired by Gandhi's writings. Nelson Mandela, black nationalist leader and first black president of South Africa; Lech Walesa, leader of the Polish labor union Solidarity and former president of Poland; and Cesar Chavez, Mexican-American labor leader, were all influenced by Gandhi's beliefs. Several Nobel Peace Prize winners such as the Dalai Lama of Tibet and Aung San Suu Kyi of Myanmar have stated their debt to him. Gandhi continues to be an inspiration to people who struggle for peace, justice, and nonviolence around the globe.

1. What is the main idea of the paragraph?
   a. Gandhi's belief in passive resistance has influenced many world leaders.
   b. Gandhi was awarded the Nobel Peace Prize.
   c. Martin Luther King, Jr., was inspired by Gandhi's writings.

2. The phrase *passive resistance* in the fourth sentence means
   a. inspirational writings
   b. resisting injustice in a nonviolent way
   c. fight for independence

3. Who was the first black president of South Africa?
   a. Mohandas Gandhi
   b. Nelson Mandela
   c. Cesar Chavez

4. Cesar Chavez was
   a. the president of Mexico
   b. a Tibetan religious leader
   c. a Mexican-American labor leader

Be an Active Reader

A. Discuss these questions in small groups.

    1. An idiom is a group of words that does not have the same meaning as any of the separate words in the group. For example, the idiom *to be hot under the collar* means to be angry. What are some examples of idioms in your native language? What do they mean?

    2. A proverb is a short, well-known statement that gives advice about life. A popular proverb in the United States is *A penny saved is a penny earned.* This means that it is important to save money. What are some examples of proverbs in your culture? What do they mean?

B. Turn to the article on pages 102 and 103. Read the title of the article and the headings in color. Can you guess what the article will be about?

Vocabulary Preview

The words in the box are boldfaced in the article. Work with a partner and do the exercise that follows.

> **Words to Watch**
>
> | | | | | | |
> |---|---|---|---|---|---|
> | advice | magical | punished | make up | barber | crocodile |
> | ancient | wagon | weapon | dozen | journalist | |

C. Complete each of the following sentences with the correct word from the box. If you need help, read the sentence in the article where the word appears and think about how it is used. Be sure to use the correct form of the word.

    1. We screamed when we saw the _____ open its big mouth.

    2. Guns and knives are examples of _____.

    3. My grandmother likes to give me _____ about how to dress and act.

    4. I put the newspapers in a _____ and pulled it to the recycling center.

    5. Do you believe these spices have _____ powers?

    6. I had an argument with my friend last week. I hope we _____ soon.

    7. My brother went to the new _____ on Main Street to get his hair cut.

    8. I bought a _____ eggs at the grocery store.

    9. If you commit a crime, you will be _____.

    10. The _____ Egyptians built huge pyramids.

    11. The _____ wrote an interesting article for the *New York Times*.

Idioms and Proverbs

1   If you say, "The cat is out of the bag" instead of "The secret is given away," you're using an idiom. As with other idioms, the meaning of "The cat is out of the bag" is different from the actual meaning of the words. Most languages have lots of idioms. "An apple a day keeps the doctor away" is a proverb. Proverbs are old but familiar sayings that usually give **advice**. Both idioms and proverbs are part of our daily speech. Many idioms and proverbs are very old and have interesting histories. See how many of these sayings you know.

"An apple a day keeps the doctor away."

2   This proverb comes from the **ancient** Romans, who believed the apple had **magical** powers to cure illness. In fact, apples are filled with vitamin C, protein, natural sugars, copper, and iron. They do promote health. The proverb means that eating lots of apples will help keep you healthy.

"Jump on the bandwagon"

3   In the past, it was common for musical bands to travel around the United States on **wagons**. The band played music to announce a parade or political speech. To show their support, people jumped onto the wagon and joined the musicians. Today, this idiom means to support a popular belief or idea. It usually refers to someone who hopes to benefit from supporting another person's idea.

"Saved by the bell"

4   In seventeenth-century England, a guard at Windsor Castle was accused of falling asleep at his post. He claimed that it was not true. He said he had not fallen asleep, and he could prove it. He said he was awake and had heard the church bell ring thirteen times at midnight. The people in the town believed the guard, and he was not **punished**. Today this idiom means to be saved at the last possible moment.

"Bury the hatchet"

5   Native Americans used to bury **weapons**, like hatchets, after a fight. They buried the weapons to show that fighting had ended and enemies were now at peace. Today, the idiom means to **make up** with a friend after an argument or fight.

"A baker's dozen"

6   This idiom goes back to thirteenth-century England. At that time bakers often gave an extra loaf of bread for every twelve, or **dozen**, they sold. In other words, a baker's dozen was thirteen.

"A close shave"

7   In the past, student **barbers** learned to shave on customers. If they shaved too close, their customer might be cut or even barely escape serious injury. Today, we use this idiom to mean a narrow escape.

"Dot the i's and cross the t's"

8   Many years ago, all documents were written by hand. It was very important for clerks to write everything clearly and properly. They had to be very careful with letters like *i* and *t*, which could easily be confused. The idiom

now means to pay attention to details.

"The pen is mightier than the sword."

9   In seventeenth-century England, it was illegal to print ideas that criticized the government or disagreed with its policies. Anyone who wrote critically about the government was punished. In spite of this, **journalists** and other people printed their ideas and opinions in illegal newspapers. The proverb means that the written expression of ideas is stronger than any physical weapon.

"Raining cats and dogs"

10   In old stories from Scandinavia, dogs are associated with wind, and cats are associated with storms. This expression means it's raining very heavily.

"Crocodile tears"

11   **Crocodiles** have a reflex that causes their eyes to tear when they open their mouths. This makes it look like they are crying while they are eating the animal they killed. In fact, the crocodiles are not really sorry about killing another animal. People who cry "crocodile" tears don't really feel sorry for their actions. "Crocodile" tears are false tears.

12   As you see from reading this article, idioms and proverbs often have interesting histories. Some of these expressions are very old, but it is not common for people in modern times to know or understand their origin. However, it is always interesting to learn how these expressions came about.

Idioms and Proverbs

Idiom or Proverb	History	Meaning
"An apple a day keeps the doctor away."	Ancient Romans believed the apple had magical powers to cure illness.	Eating apples will keep you healthy.

AFTER YOU READ

After you have read "Idioms and Proverbs," complete the following exercises.

Check Your Comprehension

See how much you can remember from "Idioms and Proverbs." If you are not sure of the answer, you can refer to the article.

A. True or False? Write T (True) or F (False) next to each of the following statements. If a statement is false, correct it to make it true.

____ 1. The meaning of an idiom is the same as the real meaning of the words.

____ 2. Proverbs are well-known sayings that give advice.

____ 3. Many idioms and proverbs come from long ago.

____ 4. Proverbs and idioms are the same thing.

____ 5. Both idioms and proverbs are part of daily speech.

B. Answer the questions with *yes* or *no*.

1. If it's raining cats and dogs, would you take an umbrella? ____

2. If you bury the hatchet, are you still angry with your friend? ____

3. When you shed crocodile tears about something, are you truly sorry? ____

4. If you buy cookies and get a baker's dozen, do you get thirteen cookies? ____

C. Complete the conversations with the appropriate idiom or proverb from the article.

1. **A:** The article she wrote about the political situation changed people's minds.

   B: I guess it's true that _____.

2. **A:** I listened to the weather report. I guess we'll have to cancel the picnic.

   B: You're right. It's supposed to _____.

3. **A:** You eat so much fruit!

   B: My grandmother said, "_____."

4. **A:** I'm so glad the class ended before the teacher called on me.

   B: You were _____.

5. **A:** Marianne said Sunshine Industries is doing so well that she invested money in the company.

   B: She _____.

6. **A:** I hear Frank and Peter aren't fighting anymore.

   B: Good! After all these years they have finally _____.

D. Work in small groups. Each of the situations below illustrates one of the idioms in the article. Read the situations and identify the idiom it illustrates.

1. A girl was caught cheating on an exam. She apologized, but she wasn't really sorry about what happened. She just wanted sympathy.

   _____

2. Two neighbors had been angry at each other for years. Another neighbor finally convinced them to make up, and now they are friends again.

   _____

3. A little boy didn't look before he crossed a busy street. He was almost hit by a bus. Luckily, the bus driver saw the little boy just in time and put on the brakes.

   _____

Test Your Vocabulary

E. Use context clues from the article to write a definition of each word. Then look up the words in a dictionary and compare the definitions.

1. advice _____

2. ancient _____

3. magical _____

4. wagon _____

5. punished _____

6. weapon _____

7. make up _____

8. dozen _____

9. barber _____

10. journalist _____

Sum It Up

Reread "Idioms and Proverbs" and complete this one-paragraph summary of the article. Include one specific example in your summary.

Many idioms and proverbs have an interesting history. _____

_____

_____

_____

_____

Express Your Ideas

A. Discuss these questions in small groups.

1. Review the meaning of the proverb *The pen is mightier than the sword.* Then think about the meaning of another proverb: *Actions speak louder than words.* What do you think this proverb means? How are the two proverbs different?

2. What is your favorite proverb? Can you think of an example from your life that proves or disproves the proverb?

3. Does your native language have a lot of idioms? What are some of the most common idioms in your native language? What do they mean?

4. Do you think proverbs and idioms reflect the ideas of the culture they come from? Can you think of any examples to support your idea?

B. Choose one of the questions above and write a paragraph about it.

_____

_____

_____

_____

_____

Explore The Web

Benjamin Franklin was one of the Founding Fathers of the United States and one of America's greatest citizens. In addition to being an inventor, statesman, scientist, philosopher, musician, and economist, Franklin was a printer. One of his most famous publications was called *Poor Richard's Almanack.* Franklin wrote many proverbs that he printed in the *Almanack.* Use the Internet to gather information about Franklin and *Poor Richard's Almanack.*

1. Make a list of four of Franklin's proverbs that you like. Explain each proverb in your own words. Use the proverbs and your paraphrases to make a poster. Your poster should include Franklin's original proverbs, your explanations, and an illustration.

_____

_____

_____

_____

2. Pretend you are writing your own almanac with proverbs. Make up four proverbs that you would include in your almanac. Share your proverbs with your classmates. Then decide which three proverbs are the most popular in your class.

Become a Better Reader

Do your best to read the following text and answer the questions in three minutes. Then turn to page 169 to check your answers. Finally, turn to the chart on page 170 to keep track of your progress.

The Loch Ness Monster: Real or Imaginary?

1   Is the Loch Ness Monster a real animal, or is it just a story? Thousands of people have reported seeing a strange creature in Loch Ness, a long lake in northern Scotland. Most have described it as a huge swimming reptile with a long neck and tail and rounded back.

2   Early evidence of such a creature exists on stone carvings dating back to more than 1,500 years ago. These pictures show an animal that looks something like a long swimming elephant. During the nineteenth century many people reported seeing a strange sea animal in Loch Ness. In 1933, a road was built along the lake, and there was an increase in the number of people who said they saw the creature. The sightings continue today. Some photos have been taken of the animal, but experts say they are too unclear or they are not real. However, boats on Loch Ness have noticed sound waves of a large moving object under the surface of the water.

3   Hundreds of newspaper and television reporters have studied the story of the Loch Ness Monster. In addition, many of the witnesses who have said they saw a strange animal in Loch Ness have been highly respected people, including scientists, priests, teachers, and police officers. However, despite these efforts, there is still no clear proof that the monster really exists. The legend of the Loch Ness Monster is a mystery that continues to attract attention.

1. The Loch Ness Monster is a strange-looking creature that supposedly lives in
   a. a lake in Scotland
   b. a boat
   c. a swimming pool

2. Stories about the Loch Ness Monster
   a. began in 1933
   b. have existed for centuries
   c. stopped in the twenty-first century

3. Photographs of the creature of Loch Ness
   a. are clear and convincing
   b. are mostly unclear or considered unreal
   c. have all disappeared

4. The people who reported seeing a strange animal in Loch Ness
   a. are all journalists
   b. are all mysterious
   c. include respected professionals

Have Some Fun

Work with a partner. Look at the ads. Use the context of the ad to guess the meaning of the underlined idioms. Write the meaning on the line. Then, compare your definitions with those of another pair of students.

1. _____

Cell Service Direct

We make it easy to <u>keep in touch</u>!

Call us today to learn about our **new, low rates**.

Savings today are just a phone call away! **222-666-7235**

2. _____

For <u>thumbs-up service</u>, come to **STAR**—where you'll always be happy with the service on your car! Call us today and put your car cares away.

222-333-5141

Conveniently located at the corner of West Juniper and Cedar Streets.

3. _____

> Try out our NEW, improved
> vegetable chopper
> on sale now for only $15.95.
>
> ### *Order today!*
> ### *Call 222-555-2979!*
>
> *If you are not 100% satisfied, return your*
> *vegetable chopper within fifteen days and*
> *we'll refund your money, no questions asked.*

TRY IT OUT! MONEY BACK GUARANTEE!

4. _____

🌀 *COMFORT HOTEL*

> *Spend the night with us,*
> *and breakfast is <u>on the house</u>!*

Comfort Hotel offers weekend specials, like free breakfast
and one night at half-price all summer.

5. _____

WE <u>SEE EYE TO EYE</u> WITH YOU.

Glasses should be affordable and fashionable.
Come on in to **Masses of Glasses**
today for the largest selection of frames
and the best prices in town.

141 Pine Street

CHAPTER 6

Put Things in Order
Recognizing Sequence

Source: PEANUTS reprinted by permission of United Feature Syndicate, Inc.

Look at the pictures. They are all from one comic strip, but they are not in the right order. Work with a partner.

1. Think about the pictures. Discuss them with a partner and number them 1–4, so they tell the story in the right order.

2. Join another pair of students and compare your decisions about the order.

3. What clues did you use to help you put the pictures in order?

When you looked at the pictures, you had to think about the order of events in the comic strip. This is called **sequencing**. In the same way, when you read something, you often need to understand the order of events. In other words, you need to learn to recognize sequence.

Sharpen Your Reading Skills

RECOGNIZING SEQUENCE

Most things that you read have some kind of order or organization. Understanding how a passage is organized will help you understand and remember the passage better. It will also help you locate information in the reading more easily.

One way that authors organize information is to sequence events according to what happened first, second, third, and so on. Sometimes authors use signal words to help you recognize the sequence of events. Other times, you will have to consider the content in order to recognize the sequence.

Signal Words

after	finally	second
another	first	today
as soon as	last	then
at last	later	when
at the same time	next	while
before	now	

Also look for *dates, seasons, days of the week,* and *times.*

A. Read the following paragraphs. As you read, think about the order of events. Then, number the details that follow each paragraph in the correct time order.

1.   M&M candies have had a very colorful life. When they were first introduced in 1941, M&Ms came in red, yellow, green, brown, orange, and violet. By 1949, tan had replaced violet. In 1995, the company decided to remove tan and replace it with blue. In 2002, the company announced another change. They added another new color: purple. Why purple, you may ask? Masterfoods USA, owner of the M&M Company, organized a contest called the Global Color Vote. Ten million people from around the world participated in the contest. They voted by phone, by mail, and on the Internet. Purple won. Aqua came in second, and pink was in last

(Continued on next page.)

place. If the past tells us anything about the future, we can look forward to new colors of M&Ms in the years to come.

___ Tan replaced violet.

___ Another new color, purple, was added.

___ M&Ms came in red, yellow, green, brown, orange, and violet.

___ Tan was replaced with blue.

2.   Did you know that ice cream was first eaten in China around 2000 B.C.? It was a favorite food of royalty. From China, ice cream moved west along trade routes to what is now Italy. By the sixteenth century, it was the most popular dessert in Florence, Italy, and chefs began making it in many different flavors. After that, ice cream's popularity spread all over Europe and later to North America. Today, ice cream remains as popular as it ever was in history.

___ Ice cream moved west along trade routes to Italy.

___ Ice cream was first eaten in China.

___ Today, ice cream remains very popular.

___ Ice cream's popularity spread all over Europe and later to North America.

3.   The snowplows in Toronto were very busy this weekend. The snow started falling on Friday night. It was light at first, but by Saturday morning, there were 10 inches of the white stuff on the ground. Heavy snow continued to fall and at 5 P.M., there were over 2 feet of snow. At 7 P.M., major roads were closed, and soon the airport was closed, too. It didn't stop snowing until late Sunday morning. This was the worst snowstorm of the winter.

___ The roads and airport were closed.

___ By Saturday morning, there were 10 inches of snow.

___ The snow began to fall on Friday night.

___ The snow stopped on Sunday morning.

4.   One of the oldest dreams of humans is to fly across the sky like birds. An early attempt at flying was in hot air balloons. The first people to fly in a hot air balloon were Jean-François Pilatre de Rozier and François Laurent. They took their trip into the skies on November 21, 1783. In the late 1800s, Alberto Santos-Dumont, a Brazilian, constructed airships with gasoline-powered engines. Then, on December 17, 1903, Orville and Wilber Wright made aviation history with their first real plane flight.

___ Alberto Santos-Dumont made airships with gasoline-powered engines.

___ Orville and Wilber Wright flew the first real plane.

___ Jean-François Pilatre de Rozier and François Laurent flew in a hot air balloon.

5.   In 1912, a new steamship called the *Titanic* set out from Southampton, England. The *Titanic* was part of England's White Star Line and it was on its way to New York City. There were 2,227 enthusiastic passengers and crewmembers on board for the history-making trip. The "unsinkable" ocean liner was shipwrecked in the early hours of April 15, shortly after it hit an iceberg in the North Atlantic Ocean. The ship sank and about 1,000 of its passengers and crew drowned.

____ The *Titanic* sank along with most of its passengers.

____ The *Titanic* hit an iceberg in the North Atlantic.

____ 2,227 passengers and crew set off on the *Titanic* for New York City.

6.   The cellist Yo-yo Ma was born in 1955 in Paris, France. His father was a musicologist of Chinese descent who had left China in the 1930s. By 1960, Ma began giving public recitals in Paris, and it became apparent that he was a musical prodigy. In 1963, Yo-yo Ma and his family moved to New York City. At the age of nine, Yo-yo Ma began attending the Julliard School of Music, one of the most competitive schools of music in the world. Just one year later, Ma performed at the prestigious Carnegie Hall. In later years, Ma studied at Harvard University. Yo-yo Ma is one of our most brilliant musicians, and probably one of the best cellists of all time. He continues to perform as a soloist with many of the world's best orchestras.

____ Yo-yo Ma attended the Julliard School of Music.

____ Ma gave public recitals in Paris.

____ He performs as a soloist with many of the world's best orchestras.

____ Ma performed at Carnegie Hall.

____ Ma studied at Harvard University.

B. **Work with a partner. Read the following paragraph. You will notice that two of the sentences are not in the correct time order. On the next page, rewrite the paragraph so all the sentences follow a logical sequence.**

Throughout history, people have found it necessary to do mathematical computations and keep accounts. In early times, they used groups of sticks or stones to help make calculations. Another example is the first machine that would do calculations and print out results, which Charles Babbage designed in 1830. Then the abacus was developed in China around A.D. 1200. These simple methods represent the beginnings of data processing. As computational needs became more complicated, people developed more advanced technologies. One example is the first simple adding machine that Blaise Pascal developed in 1642. Today, of course, we have the computer to perform all kinds of advanced mathematical computations. In the middle of the twentieth century, researchers at the University of Pennsylvania built the first electronic computer.

_____

_____

(Continued on next page.)

_____

_____

_____

_____

_____

_____

c. Choose one of the topics in the Sharpen Your Reading Skills activities on pages 111–113. On a separate piece of paper draw a series of pictures that show the sequence of events. Label the pictures. Then, share your drawings with your classmates.

 TIP Look for clues such as dates and signal words to help you figure out the sequence of events in a reading.

Test Your Skills

Read each paragraph and answer the four questions that follow. The first question is about the main idea of the passage. The second is a vocabulary question that you should be able to answer using context clues. The third and fourth questions test your understanding of details in the passage.

A.   People have always been interested in sending signals, or messages, to each other. Over the years, the transmission of signals has become more and more powerful. The earliest way to send a message without personally delivering it was to give a signal that could be seen from far away. Some early examples include fire signals, smoke signals, and flag waving. In the 1830s, Samuel Morse invented the telegraph, which sent electrical signals along a wire. People sent messages in a code of long and short beeps, called Morse code. In 1901, the first radio message was sent across the Atlantic by Italian inventor Guglielmo Marconi. He proved that it is possible to communicate with electrical signals. Today, messages can be turned into light pulses as well as electrical signals. Tiny glass tubes called optical fibers carry light pulses. Today, fiber optic technology uses light to carry sound signals farther, faster, and more efficiently than ever before.

1. What is the main idea of the paragraph?
    a. Fiber optic technology uses light to carry sound signals.
    b. The transmission of signals has become more powerful.
    c. The history of signals began in 1901.
    d. Transmitting signals is the basis of technology.

2. *Optical fibers* are
  a. small glass tubes
  b. electrical signals
  c. a pair of glasses
  d. smoke signals

3. The paragraph does *not* mention
  a. who sent the first radio message across the Atlantic
  b. problems with fiber optic technology
  c. early ways of sending signals
  d. when the telegraph was invented

4. Which sequence of events is correct?
  a. smoke signals, radio, telegraph, fiber optics
  b. fiber optics, smoke signals, telegraph, radio
  c. smoke signals, fiber optics, telegraph, radio
  d. smoke signals, telegraph, radio, fiber optics

B.   As the first female medical doctor in the United States, Elizabeth Blackwell serves as a role model for women trying to overcome obstacles. Elizabeth Blackwell was born in Bristol, England, on February 3, 1821, and immigrated to New York City about ten years later. As a young woman, Elizabeth dreamed of becoming a medical doctor. She applied to several schools, but because she was female, only one would take her: Geneva Medical College in New York. She graduated at the top of her class in 1849. However, her problems were not over. After she graduated, Blackwell went to London to learn more about medicine. She came back to the United States in 1851 to start working as a doctor, but no one would hire her, again because she was a woman. However, Elizabeth Blackwell was determined to practice medicine, so she started her own infirmary, or hospital. Today, Elizabeth Blackwell's life remains an inspiration to many young women all over the world.

1. What is the main idea of the paragraph?
  a. Elizabeth Blackwell started her own infirmary.
  b. Elizabeth Blackwell is a role model for women trying to overcome obstacles.
  c. Elizabeth Blackwell is the first woman to overcome difficulties.

2. The word *infirmary* means
  a. hospital
  b. sickness
  c. school

3. When did Blackwell graduate from medical school?
  a. 1821
  b. 1849
  c. 1841

4. Which sequence of events in Blackwell's life is correct?
   a. born in 1821, immigrated to New York City, graduated from medical school, started her own infirmary, studied in London
   b. born in 1821, immigrated to New York City, graduated from medical school, studied in London, started her own infirmary
   c. born in 1821, started her own infirmary, immigrated to New York City, graduated from medical school, studied in London

C.   Much of the history of the state of Arizona has been shaped by its scarce water supply. From A.D. 300 to A.D. 1450, Native Americans living there solved the problem of inadequate water supply by building canals to bring water to their fields. Their canal system covered about 500 miles, and may have served as many as 50,000 people at a time. The Native Americans lived there for more than 1,000 years but left the area for unknown reasons. A century ago, when new settlers came to Arizona, they were challenged by the harsh desert environment with its lack of water. Luckily, they discovered the old Native American canals and connected the canals to a river. This way they were able to bring water to their crops, such as corn and wheat. Then, in the early 1900s, engineers in Arizona built several dams to store water for the crops. The water storage and delivery system brought new life to the land. More than any other single factor, this system influenced the development of Arizona.

1. What is the main idea of the paragraph?
   a. Arizona's history has been influenced by its scarce water supply.
   b. Arizona has the most efficient dams in the United States.
   c. New settlers in Arizona discovered the old Native American canals.

2. The word *crops* means
   a. water storage systems
   b. canals to bring water
   c. plants that are grown for food

3. Which sequence of events is correct?
   a. Native Americans built canals, settlers connected old canals to a river, engineers built dams
   b. engineers built dams, Native Americans built canals, settlers connected old canals to a river
   c. Native Americans built canals, engineers built dams, settlers connected old canals to a river

4. What challenge faced settlers in Arizona?
   a. Inadequate water supply
   b. Lack of leadership
   c. Disagreements with the Native Americans over water
   d. Inadequate funds to build dams

Be an Active Reader

BEFORE YOU READ

A. In small groups, read and check the statements you agree with.

_____ **1.** Parents tell folktales to teach lessons to their children.

_____ **2.** Folktales help people learn and understand the customs of their culture.

_____ **3.** Folktales are told to explain the wonders of nature, like volcanoes.

_____ **4.** Folktales reveal a lot about the culture of the people who tell them.

_____ **5.** People have only recently begun to tell folktales.

Vocabulary Preview

The words in the box are boldfaced in the story on pages 118 and 119. Work with a partner and do the exercise that follows.

> **Words to Watch**
>
> fierce   frequent   solution   island   blame   warning   beg

B. Match the words in the left column with the correct definitions in the right column. Write the letter of the correct definition on the line.

_____ **1.** island

_____ **2.** solution

_____ **3.** warning

_____ **4.** fierce

_____ **5.** beg

_____ **6.** frequent

_____ **7.** blame

a. to urgently ask for something

b. advice that prepares you for something bad or dangerous

c. to say that someone is responsible for something bad

d. happening often

e. a piece of land surrounded by water

f. very angry, violent, and ready to attack

g. a way of dealing with a difficult situation

Set a Purpose

The following story is an old Samoan folktale. Look at the map of Tutuila Island in Samoa. It shows where the story takes place. The two large mountains, Matafao and Pioa, are known as the Two Brothers. The folktale explains how they were created.

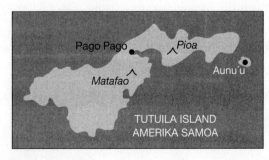

Write three questions that you hope the story answers.

As you read the story, make predictions about what you think will happen next.

The Story of the Two Brothers

1   Long ago, a man had two sons. He loved both children very much. One son he named Matafao; the other, Pioa. As small boys, they argued constantly. As they grew older, their fights became ever **fiercer** and more **frequent**.

2   Time passed. The father grew old. Tired of listening to his sons fight with each other, he began to lose hope. He knew the time was near when he would leave them. What would happen to his angry children?

> Make a prediction. What do you think will happen next?

3   One day their father called Pioa and Matafao to him. This is what he told them: "My heart is heavy. It seems you cannot love each other as brothers should. In fact, every time you are together, one of you starts a fight. The only **solution** I can see is to separate you forever. Therefore, from today, you will live apart from each other. Pioa, you will live in the east," he said. "Matafao, you will live in the west. Perhaps the sea will be wide enough to keep you from fighting when I could not."

4   And then he added, "If either of you starts a fight, you will be turned into stone on the spot where you stand."

5   Soon the old man died.

6   Although the two brothers could not seem to love each other, they both loved their father. Their grief for him was great. In fact, they were so sad they could not eat. If their sadness had continued they surely would have died, too.

7   With the passage of time, grief lessens. So it was with them. The two brothers began to be happy again. They decided to have a feast. They would roast a whole pig and many chickens to feed the whole community. They would boil taro, a root vegetable, and bake a big cake.

8   Matafao and Pioa ate well at their feast. In fact, Matafao may have eaten a little too well. He decided to climb a cliff and look over his beautiful green **island**.

9   At that moment, high above their heads, a bird picked up a rock. The bird raised his great wings and flew up to the sky. When a strong wind blew, the rock slipped from his claws. The rock fell down the cliff and hit Pioa on the top of his head.

> Make a prediction. What do you think will happen next?

10   Pioa looked up. He became angry and **blamed** his brother, not the bird or the wind.

11   "It is your fault, Matafao!" Pioa screamed. "You threw the rock!" Then, he picked up a stone and threw it at his brother.

12   At those angry and unjust words, Matafao also got angry and threw some rocks. Rocks began to fly between the brothers, just as when a volcano erupts. Only then did they remember their father's **warning**, "Whoever starts another fight will be turned into stone."

13   Too late they found their father's words were true. Their legs had hardened and turned to stone.

14   Matafao realized then that fighting with his brother was wrong. He stopped fighting and **begged** his brother to stop, too. But Pioa was too angry, and he continued to fight.

15   "Stop, Brother. I beg you," Matafao pleaded again. When he saw that Pioa was ignoring him, Matafao fought back.

> Make a prediction. What do you think will happen next?

16   It was at that moment that Pioa and Matafao became the mountains known as the Two Brothers. Pioa was humbled by his own wrongdoings. So, he became the smaller of the two mountains. The dark cloud that hovers over his head brings rain to the islands. "The Story of the Two Brothers" is still told to Samoan children. It teaches them several morals. For example, it reminds Samoan children to love one another. It also teaches that fighting is not a good way to resolve problems.

AFTER YOU READ

After you have read "The Story of the Two Brothers," complete the following exercises.

Check Your Comprehension

See how much you can remember from "The Story of the Two Brothers." If you are not sure of the answer, you can refer to the story.

A. True or False? Write T (True) or F (False) next to each of the following statements. If a statement is false, correct it to make it true.

___ 1. Matafao and Pioa got along well as children.

___ 2. Matafao and Pioa were very sad when their father died.

___ 3. A bird bit Pioa on the head.

___ 4. Matafao finally realized that fighting with his brother was wrong.

___ 5. Pioa became a taller mountain than his brother.

___ 6. *The Story of the Two Brothers* is never told anymore.

___ 7. One moral of the story is that fighting is not a good way to resolve problems.

B. Look at the pictures that go with the story. They are not in the correct order. Number the pictures so they follow the order of the story.

_____   _____   _____

_____   _____   _____

Now write a short description of each picture.

An old man is talking to his two sons.

1. _____

2. _____

3. _____

4. _____

5. _____

6. _____

C. Act out "The Story of the Two Brothers" with two of your classmates. Choose one person to be Matafao, another to be Pioa, and the third to be their father.

Test Your Vocabulary

D. Use context clues to figure out the general meaning of the underlined words. Don't worry about getting an exact definition. Be satisfied with a general meaning.

1. He decided to climb a <u>cliff</u> and look over his lush green island.

   _____

2. Their <u>grief</u> for him was great. In fact, they were so sad they could not eat.

   _____

3. They would boil <u>taro</u>, a root vegetable, and bake a big cake.

   _____

4. They decided to host a <u>feast</u>. They would roast a whole pig and many chickens to feed the whole community.

   _____

5. "The Story of the Two Brothers" has several <u>morals</u>. For example, it reminds Samoan children to love one another. It also teaches that fighting is not a good way to resolve problems.

   _____

6. "The only solution I can see is to <u>separate</u> you forever. Therefore, from today, you will live apart from each other."

   _____

7. "Stop, Brother. I <u>beg</u> you," Matafao pleaded again.

   _____

E. Choose the word that best completes each of the following sentences. Be sure to use the correct form of the word.

> beg   frequent   solution
> blame   island   warning
> fierce

1. Don't _____ me for the accident. It wasn't my fault.

2. The fight was _____ and bloody.

3. Can you find a good _____ for the problem?

4. I _____ them to stop fighting.

5. This is your last _____. Do not be late for class again.

6. We spent our vacation on a beautiful _____ in the Pacific Ocean.

7. Our teacher gives _____ quizzes.

Sharpen Your Vocabulary Skills

WORD PARTS

Suffixes

You learned in Chapter 3 that many English words are made up of several word parts: *prefixes*, *roots*, and *suffixes*. You can use suffixes to figure out the meaning of an unfamiliar word.

> A **suffix** is a word part that is added to the end of a word. A suffix can change the meaning of a word, or it can change the way it is used in a sentence. For example, when the suffix **-er** is added to the verb **teach** it becomes the noun **teacher** (*someone who teaches*).

English has several suffixes that mean *someone who*. For example, from the verb *run* we can make *runner*, someone who runs, by adding *-er*; from *sail* we can make *sailor*, someone who sails, by adding *-or*. Study the chart to learn about the suffixes that mean *someone who*.

Suffixes That Mean *someone who*	
Suffix	Example
-er	teacher
-or	governor
-ian	mathematician
-ist	pianist

Write a definition for each of the following words. You may need to refer to a dictionary.

1. computer programmer _____

   _____

2. cyclist _____

   _____

3. geneticist _____

   _____

4. theologian _____

   _____

5. physicist _____

   _____

6. economist _____

   _____

7. electrician _____

   _____

8. translator _____

   _____

9. librarian _____

   _____

10. investigator _____

    _____

English has many other suffixes. Study the chart on the next page to learn some common suffixes. Learning the suffixes will help you expand your vocabulary.

Common Suffixes		
Suffix	Meaning	Examples
Adjectives		
-able, -ible	*capable of, having a particular quality*	manageable, comfortable, reversible, responsible
-ful	*full of*	beautiful, harmful
-less	*without something*	childless, careless, endless
-ous, -ious	*full of, having the qualities of*	dangerous, furious
-y	*full of or covered with something, tending to do something*	angry, hairy, curly, sleepy
Nouns		
-ism	*action or practice of, belief or theory*	Buddhism, capitalism, criticism
-ment	*the act or result of doing something*	government, development
-ness	*condition, quality, state of being*	sadness, softness
-ology	*the study or science of something*	geology, technology
Adverb		
-ly	*in a particular way*	slowly, constantly, hourly

Sum It Up

Make a list of the main events in the story. You may want to refer to your descriptions of the pictures on page 120. Then, in your own words, tell what the folktale "The Story of the Two Brothers" is about.

_____

_____

_____

_____

_____

_____

Express Your Ideas

A. Discuss these questions in small groups.

   1. Why do you think folktales can be found in every culture around the world?
   2. What is your favorite folktale? Why?
   3. Do you agree that folktales give important messages? Why or why not?
   4. If you could write your own folktale, what would it be about?

B. Do one of the following:

   1. Think about how "The Story of the Two Brothers" ends. Then, try to come up with a different ending. For example, what could have happened if the brothers had made up instead of fighting? Write your new ending.
   2. Choose one of the questions above and write a paragraph about it.

_____

_____

_____

_____

_____

_____

_____

_____

_____

_____

_____

_____

Explore the Web

Do some research on the Web about a folktale from your native country. Make a list of the events in the story or draw several pictures that show the sequence of events in the folktale. Tell the folktale to your classmates or act it out with several of your classmates.

Become a Better Reader

Do your best to read the following text and answer the questions in three minutes. Then turn to page 169 to check your answers for accuracy. Finally, turn to the chart on page 170 to keep track of your progress.

Laser Eye Surgery

1 It is not unusual to hear people who wear eyeglasses say, "I can't find my glasses!" Another commonly heard comment is, "I lost a contact! Please help me find it!" It seems that whether people wear eyeglasses or contact lenses, they have trouble finding them. Perhaps this type of problem will occur less often now that medical science can make eyeglasses and contact lenses less necessary.

2 New medical advances in the field of laser eye surgery may help correct some common eye problems. Both nearsightedness and farsightedness can now be corrected through surgery. People who are nearsighted can see clearly only when something is close up. They do not see well when things are far away. Those who are farsighted can see well far away, at a distance, but not close up. Laser surgery can now correct these types of vision problems. The surgery takes only a few minutes, and the recovery period is not long.

3 With this surgery, patients no longer have to wear eyeglasses or use contact lenses. People who have had the surgery report that they feel a new freedom in their lives since they can see well, and they don't have to depend on glasses or contacts. However, not all people can have the surgery. An examination with an ophthalmologist, or eye specialist, can determine whether laser surgery would be possible.

1. People who wear eyeglasses and contact lenses
   a. often have trouble finding them
   b. often cause trouble, and should be more careful
   c. are afraid of medical advances

2. Laser eye surgery can correct vision problems for people who are
   a. farsighted
   b. nearsighted
   c. farsighted and nearsighted

3. The recovery period after laser eye surgery is
   a. only a few minutes
   b. not very long
   c. a long period of time

4. Many people are happy with laser eye surgery because
   a. they experience better vision and a feeling of freedom
   b. it's good for everyone and for every type of eye problem
   c. they can wear better eyeglasses and contacts

Have Some Fun

A. Folktales usually have a message. The message of "The Story of the Two Brothers" is *Fighting is not a good way to resolve problems.* Read the following folktale from India. What is the message? Write it on the line.

_____

Three Fish

A Tale from India

1   Three fish lived in a pond. One was named Plan Ahead, another was Think Fast, and the third was named Wait and See. One day they heard a fisherman say that he was going to cast his net in their pond the next day.

2   Plan Ahead said, "I'm swimming down the river tonight!" Think Fast said, "I'm sure I'll come up with a plan." Wait and See lazily said, "I just can't think about it now!"

3   When the fisherman cast his nets, Plan Ahead was long gone. But Think Fast and Wait and See were caught!

4   Think Fast quickly rolled his belly up and pretended to be dead. "Oh, this fish is no good!" said the fisherman, and threw him safely back into the water. But, Wait and See ended up in the fish market.

5   That is why they say, "In times of danger, when the net is cast, plan ahead or plan to think fast."

B. Work with a group of three or four students. Make up a folktale to tell your classmates. Follow these steps.

1. Think of a message you want to teach in the folktale and write it on the following line.

_____

(Continued on next page.)

2. Make a list of the characters in the folktale. Your characters can be people or animals.

   _____

   _____

   _____

   _____

3. Choose a time and place for your story.

   _____

   _____

4. Write a title.

   _____

5. Make a list of events in the story. Be sure to put the events in the correct time order.

   _____

   _____

   _____

   _____

6. Draw a series of pictures to go with the story.

7. Choose someone from your group to tell the folktale to the class.

8. Take a class survey to see which folktale is the most interesting.

CHAPTER 7

Believe It or Not
Fact vs. Opinion

Make yourself at home at Wellsword Inn!

Our beautiful, historic inn is the best place to stay in Elmsford, Virginia. Built in 1845, Wellsword Inn is filled with antique furniture, oriental rugs, and fine pieces of art. From our spiral staircase to our stained-glass windows, you'll know you are entering a very special place. We are located at the end of a quiet street, overlooking the sea. You'll be impressed with our delicious breakfasts, outstanding hospitality, and personal attention. All rooms are air-conditioned and include cable TV, Internet access, telephone, and king-size beds.

Call now to make your reservation: (800) 555-1234.

Look at the advertisement for Wellsword Inn. Discuss it with a partner.

1. Make a list of the facts in the advertisement.

Wellsword Inn is located in Elmsford, Virginia.

_____

_____

_____

_____

2. Make a list of the opinions in the advertisement.

Wellsword Inn is the best place to stay in Elmsford.

_____

_____

_____

_____

3. Compare your lists with those of another pair of students.

When you looked at the advertisement, you decided which information was fact and which was opinion. Whenever you read, you need to figure out whether you are reading something that is a fact or an opinion.

Sharpen Your Reading Skills

DISTINGUISHING FACTS FROM OPINIONS

Learning to understand the difference between facts and opinions is a valuable skill.

Think about this statement:

- _There are too many words in the English language._

Do you agree or disagree with the statement?   ☐ Agree   ☐ Disagree

It is possible to agree or disagree with the statement because it is an **opinion.** You cannot prove whether there are too many words in the English language or not. Opinions are beliefs that cannot be proven.

Now think about this statement:

- _The human body has 206 bones._

You can't agree or disagree with this statement because it is a **fact.** You can count the number of bones in the body to prove that there are exactly 206. Facts can be checked. They can be observed, counted, and measured. Unlike opinions, facts can be proven to be true.

- **Facts** are statements that can be proven to be true.
- **Opinions** are statements that describe someone's feelings or beliefs about a topic. They cannot be proven.

The ability to distinguish between facts and opinions will help you to make judgments about what you read.

A. Indicate whether each of the following statements is a fact or an opinion. Write *Fact* or *Opinion* on the line.

Example

___Fact___   The Nile River is the longest river in the world.

_____ 1. Washington, D.C., is the capital of the United States.

_____ 2. Blondes have more fun.

_____ 3. Children shouldn't watch more than an hour of TV a day.

_____ 4. Famous athletes make great role models for children.

_____ 5. Soccer is the most popular sport in the world.

_____ 6. South Americans are more polite than North Americans.

_____ 7. According to a government survey, 98 percent of U.S. homes have a telephone.

_____ 8. From 1952–1953, *I Love Lucy* was the most popular show on television in the United States.

_____ 9. The Beatles were the best rock band in history.

_____ 10. Turtles make great pets.

_____ 11. You should invest your money in real estate.

_____ 12. This new computer program is easy to use.

_____ 13. A triangle has three sides.

_____ 14. The sun rises in the east and sets in the west.

_____ 15. In August of 1883, the volcano on the island of Krakatoa, Indonesia erupted.

B. Now read each paragraph and the statements that follow. Circle *Fact* or *Opinion.*

1.   Chocolate, one of the most delicious foods in the world, has had a long and interesting history. It is believed that the Spanish explorer Hernan Cortes brought cacao beans from Central America to Europe in the sixteenth century. At first, chocolate was usually consumed as a hot drink. In the nineteenth century, Europeans began experimenting with making different forms of chocolate candy. Switzerland became famous for its chocolate, and today, the Swiss make the best chocolate in the world. They also eat the most chocolate in the world, about 10 kilograms annually (more than 20 pounds per person). Enjoyed all over the world, chocolate will probably continue to be immensely popular well into the future.

Fact   Opinion   **a.** Chocolate is one of the most delicious foods in the world.

Fact   Opinion   **b.** Europeans began experimenting with making different forms of chocolate candy in the nineteenth century.

Fact   Opinion   **c.** The Swiss make the best chocolate in the world.

2.   Almost everyone suffers from the common cold, with symptoms of coughing and sneezing, and almost everyone has advice about the best way to treat a cold. Some people believe in traditional cures such as chicken soup. Favorite recipes for the best chicken soup are passed down through families from generation to generation. Other people suggest drinking hot tea with lemon or honey. Hot tea is good for colds, and it's also delicious. Vinegar, garlic, and ginger are also popular folk methods to cure the symptoms of a cold. Some doctors recommend frequent doses of vitamin C. Most agree that to take care of a cold, it's a good idea to drink plenty of liquids and get plenty of rest.

Fact   Opinion   **a.** Some people believe in traditional cures such as chicken soup.

Fact   Opinion   **b.** Hot tea is good for colds, and it's also delicious.

Fact   Opinion   **c.** Some doctors recommend frequent doses of vitamin C.

3.   Laura Ingalls Wilder is one of the most famous and beloved American authors. She wrote nine books, the "Little House" series, about her childhood growing up on farms on the western frontier. Her books describe the difficult conditions for families moving west at the end of the nineteenth century. The pioneers had to build everything themselves on their farms and work together to create new towns. Not everyone survived the life there because of the long, cold winters and severe storms. Although Wilder's family faced serious problems, her books are filled with examples of kindness, love, and an optimistic spirit of adventure. Even if you are not interested in frontier life, you should read one of Wilder's wonderful books.

Fact   Opinion   **a.** Wilder wrote nine books, the "Little House" series, about her childhood growing up on farms on the western frontier.

Fact	Opinion	**b.** Her books describe the difficult conditions for families moving west at the end of the nineteenth century.
Fact	Opinion	**c.** Even if you are not interested in frontier life, you should read one of Wilder's wonderful books.

4.   Thomas Alva Edison is remembered for his many useful inventions, such as the phonograph and electric lamp, and his contributions to society. He was the most creative thinker of his time. Edison spent his childhood in Ohio and Michigan and received most of his education from his mother. He attended school for only a few months, at the age of seven. He lost his hearing at a young age possibly because of a childhood illness. As an adult, Edison lived mainly in New Jersey, where he created his inventions. Besides the phonograph and electric lamp, Edison invented alkaline batteries and electric parts for the telegraph. Another important contribution is that he developed the first electric power station. Edison founded his own company, which eventually became General Electric, one of the world's largest companies.

Fact	Opinion	**a.** Thomas Alva Edison is well known for his inventions of the phonograph and electric lamp.
Fact	Opinion	**b.** He was the most creative thinker of his time.
Fact	Opinion	**c.** Edison invented alkaline batteries and electric parts for the telegraph.

5.   *The Nutcracker* is one of the best ballets in the world. It is based on the book called *The Nutcracker and the Mouse King,* written by E. T. A. Hoffman. The music of *The Nutcracker* ballet was composed by the famous Russian composer Piotr Ilyitch Tchaikovsky. *The Nutcracker* tells the story of a young girl who receives a nutcracker doll as a holiday gift. That night, she dreams that the nutcracker has turned into a real prince. She saves the life of the prince during a fight with the Mouse King, leader of all the mice. The prince then takes her to a magic land. In this land of fantasy, they watch Russian, Spanish, Chinese, Arabian, and French dances. Finally, the girl wakes up, smiling as she remembers her beautiful dream. Many people also smile after they see this beautiful ballet.

Fact	Opinion	**a.** *The Nutcracker* is one of the best ballets in the world.
Fact	Opinion	**b.** It is based on the book called *The Nutcracker and the Mouse King,* written by E. T. A. Hoffman.
Fact	Opinion	**c.** The music of *The Nutcracker* ballet was composed by the famous Russian composer Piotr Ilyitch Tchaikovsky.

 Don't accept a statement as a fact just because it is printed in a book or because you read it on the Internet. Think about the statement. If it can't be proven, it's an opinion, not a fact.

Test Your Skills

Read each of the following paragraphs and answer the four questions that follow. The first question is about the main idea of the paragraph. The second and third questions test your understanding of details in the passage. The fourth question asks you to distinguish between fact and opinion.

A.   In recent years, honey has become a favorite food. It is often used to flavor drinks such as tea, and it is commonly used as a sweetener for desserts. It is also delicious on biscuits or toast. Some people believe that honey has special health benefits and therefore prefer to use it instead of sugar. Bees make honey from the nectar of flowers. There are different types of honey, each with a special flavor and color, depending on the kind of flower. The United States is a major producer of honey, and much of it comes from California and Florida.

1. The main idea of the paragraph is that
   a. honey is delicious
   b. the United States is a major producer of honey
   c. honey is a popular food for several reasons

2. Honey has different flavors because
   a. it has different colors
   b. it is made from different kinds of flowers
   c. it has several different uses

3. Some people prefer to use honey as a substitute for
   a. tea
   b. toast
   c. sugar

4. Which statement is an opinion?
   a. There are different types of honey.
   b. Honey is also delicious on biscuits or toast.
   c. The United States is a major producer of honey.

B.   Alaska is one of the most recent additions to the United States. In 1867, Secretary of State William H. Seward bought Alaska from Russia for $7.2 million. At that time only a few native groups of people lived in Alaska. Lots of politicians and American citizens thought Seward had made a big mistake by paying so much money for an empty piece of land. They called the purchase of Alaska "Seward's Folly," and "Seward's Icebox." When gold was discovered in Alaska in 1896, they changed their minds. Many people rushed to Alaska to search for gold. Finally, in 1959, the people of Alaska voted to enter the United States, and Alaska officially became the forty-ninth state.

1. The main idea of the paragraph is that
   a. Alaska is one of the newest states to enter the United States
   b. the purchase of Alaska was a mistake
   c. Alaska turned out to be a positive addition to the United States

2. Secretary of State Seward bought Alaska from
   a. a few native groups of people
   b. Russia
   c. the Alaskan people

3. Negative opinions toward Seward's purchase changed because of
   a. the discovery of gold
   b. the high cost of the purchase
   c. Alaska's entry as the forty-ninth state

4. Which statement is an opinion?
   a. Alaska officially became the forty-ninth state in 1959.
   b. Seward made a mistake by paying so much money for Alaska.
   c. Gold was discovered in Alaska in 1896.

C.   It doesn't matter whether you are old or young, male or female, single, married, divorced, or widowed—it is important that you do some financial planning. Financial planning is the process of figuring out how you can earn and manage your money to meet your goals in life. Personal financial planning is for everyone—not just the wealthy, and experts say that the earlier one starts thinking about it, the better. Many high schools and colleges offer courses in financial planning, and so do many adult education programs. Some of the best and most interesting courses are offered on-line. The more you know about and understand such things as taxes, insurance, and planning for your retirement, the better able you will be to make decisions that will affect your future.

1. The main idea of the paragraph is that
   a. financial planning is important for everyone to meet his or her goals
   b. high schools and colleges offer courses in financial planning
   c. financial planning is the process of managing money

2. Financial planning should begin
   a. with retirement
   b. at tax time
   c. as early as possible

3. Financial planning refers to
   a. attending adult education programs
   b. learning how to earn and manage money
   c. learning how to make good decisions

4. Which statement is an opinion?
   a. Many high schools and colleges offer courses in financial planning.
   b. Many adult education programs offer courses in financial planning.
   c. Some of the best and most interesting courses are offered on-line.

D.   Eleanor Roosevelt, the wife of U.S. president Franklin Roosevelt, was a First Lady who overcame hardship in her own life and actively promoted social causes. She was the most effective of all the First Ladies in American history. She supported civil rights for Americans of all races, and worked to advance women's rights, long before these issues became politically popular. She had her own radio program and wrote a daily newspaper article. Born in 1884, Eleanor had an unhappy childhood. Her mother teased her for being shy and frequently told her she was ugly. Her father was an alcoholic. Sometimes he would take Eleanor for a walk and then go into a bar, leaving her to sit outside. Both of her parents died when she was young, and then Eleanor was raised by her grandmother. While she was First Lady, Eleanor worked hard to help those who suffered or had a low position in society. After her husband died, Eleanor Roosevelt continued to work for social causes, and helped to write the United Nations Declaration of Human Rights.

1. The main idea of the paragraph is that
    a. Eleanor Roosevelt was a famous First Lady
    b. Eleanor Roosevelt helped to write the U.N. Declaration of Human Rights
    c. Eleanor Roosevelt was a First Lady who actively supported social causes

2. Eleanor's parents
    a. taught her about women's rights
    b. neglected her
    c. encouraged her to marry a politician

3. Eleanor Roosevelt was remarkable as a First Lady because
    a. she promoted social causes through a radio program and daily newspaper article
    b. she worked for the United Nations while her husband was president
    c. she had an unhappy childhood

4. Which statement is an opinion about Eleanor Roosevelt?
    a. She was born in 1884.
    b. She was the most effective of all the First Ladies in American history.
    c. She helped write the United Nations Declaration of Human Rights.

E.   Almost everyone loves to do crossword puzzles. A crossword puzzle is a game of words. The player is given the number of letters of a word and a hint about its meaning. The player uses these clues to fill in a puzzle with the right words. Although crossword puzzles are probably the most popular game in the world, they have a short history. The first crossword puzzle was published on December 21, 1913 in a newspaper called the New York World. It was created by a British man named Arthur Wynne. Wynne's first puzzle was in the shape of a diamond, and it didn't have any black squares. The first crossword puzzle was called a word-cross. The name later changed to cross-word and then crossword. Within 20 years, crossword puzzles began appearing in newspapers everywhere. Soon crossword puzzles became a fad. The first book of crossword puzzles was published in 1924. New books of crossword puzzles continue to be published all the time. Today, you can even find crossword puzzles on the Internet.

1. The main idea of the paragraph is that
    a. the first crossword puzzle was called a word-cross
    b. the popular game crossword puzzles have a short history
    c. crossword puzzles are a good way to improve your vocabulary

2. The first book of crossword puzzles was published
    a. twenty years ago
    b. in 1924
    c. by Arthur Wynne

3. Crossword puzzles
    a. can only be found in newspapers
    b. are difficult to find
    c. can be found in newspapers, books, and on the Internet

4. Which statement is an opinion about crossword puzzles?
    a. Everyone loves to do crossword puzzles.
    b. The first crossword puzzle was published on December 21, 1913.
    c. It was created by a British man named Arthur Wynne.

Be an Active Reader

BEFORE YOU READ

A. Work with a partner and answer these questions.

1. Do you like to watch movies? What kind of movies do you like to watch?

    ☐ Comedies
    ☐ Mysteries
    ☐ Biographies
    ☐ Action
    ☐ Romance

2. Make a list of your three favorite movies.

    _____

    _____

    _____

3. Share your list with your partner. Did you both include any of the same movies on your list?

4. Who is your favorite actor? Why? What movies has he been in? Who is your favorite actress? Why? What movies has she been in?

5. Have you ever seen any of the *Godfather* movies? If so, which one is your favorite?

B. You are going to read an essay about a famous American movie series. Look at the picture from *The Godfather.* Do you recognize the two men in the movie? Do you know their names? Why do you think the older man is standing above the younger man? What do you think their relationship is?

Vocabulary Preview

The words in the box are boldfaced in the essay on pages 140 and 141. Work with a partner and do the exercise that follows.

> **Words to Watch**
>
> admire   immigrate   patriarch   stereotype
> fictional   generations   revenge
>
> **Idioms to Watch**
>
> take over   take place   change your mind

c. Match the words and phrases in the left column with the correct definitions in the right column. Write the letter of the correct definition on the line. If you need help, read the sentence in the article where the word or phrase appears and think about how it is used.

Words

___ 1. stereotype

___ 2. revenge

___ 3. immigrate

___ 4. patriarch

___ 5. generation

___ 6. admire

___ 7. fictional

a. to enter another country in order to live there

b. the most important older man in a family

c. punishment for someone who has hurt you

d. to approve of and respect

e. referring to people in a story that is not real

f. a fixed idea or image of what a particular type of person or thing is like

g. all the people who are about the same age

Idioms

___ 1. take over

___ 2. take place

___ 3. change your mind

a. to change your opinions or decision about something

b. to get control of or become responsible for something

c. to happen

Set a Purpose

You are going to read an essay about the *Godfather* movies. Write three questions that you hope the article will answer.

1. _____

   _____

   _____

2. _____

   _____

   _____

3. _____

   _____

   _____

As you read the article, look for the answers to these questions. Write the answers in the box on the opposite page.

1. What are the *Godfather* films about?
2. What two stories are told in *Godfather II*?
3. What does Vito hope his son Michael will do?
4. What awards did the *Godfather* films win?
5. What did some critics object to about the *Godfather* films?

The Godfather: A Movie Classic

1   In the history of film, the *Godfather* movies are among the most popular of all time. The films are **admired** for their exciting story line, brilliant acting, and beautiful music. Based on the best-selling novel by Mario Puzo, the story follows the life of a **fictional** character named Vito Corleone, who **immigrated** to the United States from Italy, and the lives of his children and grandchildren.

2   The rise and fall of the Corleone family is told in three films. The first film of the trilogy, *The Godfather,* is mainly the story of the aging Vito Corleone, who is the boss, or godfather, of the family crime business, and of his youngest son Michael, who **takes over** his father's responsibilities. *Godfather II* tells two stories that **take place** at different times. One story is about Michael's life as head of the family business. The other story is about how Vito was forced to leave Italy as a child, his early life in New York, and his rise to power in organized crime (a large and powerful organization of criminals.) *Godfather III* completes the story of three **generations** of the Corleone family.

3   At the beginning of *The Godfather,* Vito Corleone is shown as a powerful **patriarch**, who is respected by his whole family. Michael has just returned from the army as a young war hero. Vito has always wanted Michael to work in a legal profession. He hopes that Michael will lead the family toward legal businesses in the future. Michael agrees with his father. He does not want to become involved in a life of crime and violence. But when someone tries to kill his father, Michael **changes his mind**. He decides to commit a crime in order to get **revenge**. Over the years Michael falls further and further into a life of crime. During the course of the next two films, *Godfather II* and *Godfather III,* Michael takes over leadership of the family and control of the huge criminal organization. He gains great wealth and power but loses his personal relationships with his family.

4   *The Godfather,* made in 1972, *Godfather II,* in 1974, and *Godfather III,* in 1990, were all successful movies. They won large audiences and great reviews. The *Godfather* characters are among the most unforgettable in American films. In addition to the famous actor Marlon Brando, who played Vito Corleone, there were important younger actors. The films starred Al Pacino as Michael, James Caan as his older

brother Sonny, Diane Keaton as his wife, Robert Duvall as the family lawyer, Robert De Niro as the young Vito, and Andy Garcia as Sonny's son. All have since become famous actors and have starred in many other movies. The *Godfather* films earned many film awards such as Oscars for Best Picture, Director, Screenplay, and Musical Score, and acting awards for Brando and De Niro.

5   The production of the *Godfather* series was very much a family affair. The creator of the films was Francis Ford Coppola, who directed and cowrote the screenplays. He chose his sister, Talia Shire, to play the character of Michael's sister. Coppola also chose his daughter Sofia to play Michael's daughter in *Godfather III*. Carmine Coppola, Francis's father, wrote the now famous *Godfather* music, together with Italian composer Nino Rota.

6   The films were box office hits, earning millions of dollars in movie theaters. However, some Italian-Americans did not like the emphasis on crime in the movies. They worried that this would reflect a negative **stereotype**. Other critics objected to the violence shown in these movies. Overall, however, the *Godfather* films have been very popular. Film critics often include *The Godfather* in lists of their top ten favorite American films. Audiences all over the world continue to enjoy the *Godfather* films.

Answers

1. _____
_____
_____

2. _____
_____
_____

3. _____
_____
_____

4. _____
_____
_____

5. _____
_____
_____

Check Your Comprehension

See how much you can remember from *"The Godfather:* A Movie Classic." If you are not sure of the answer, you can refer to the article.

A. True or False? Write T (True) or F (False) next to each of the following statements. If a statement is false, correct it to make it true.

____ **1.** The *Godfather* movies were based on a novel written by Mario Puzo.

____ **2.** The *Godfather* series has scenes in both Italy and the United States.

____ **3.** The *Godfather* movies portray several generations of the Coppola family.

____ **4.** Vito Corleone became very successful in New York.

____ **5.** Michael always wanted to have a profession like his father's.

____ **6.** Few of the *Godfather* actors are well known today.

____ **7.** Al Pacino won an Oscar for *The Godfather.*

____ **8.** Although there are happy moments in the *Godfather* movies, the films show serious problems within the Corleone family.

____ **9.** The *Godfather* movies were well liked by critics but did not sell many tickets in movie theaters.

____**10.** Michael Corleone was a war hero.

____**11.** The *Godfather* movies earned millions of dollars.

____**12.** Carmine Coppola wrote the music for the *Godfather* movies.

B. Fact or Opinion? Write *Fact* or *Opinion* next to each statement.

_____ **1.** *The Godfather* portrays the lives of Italian-American characters.

_____ **2.** The characters in the *Godfather* movies are the most memorable in American history.

_____ **3.** The *Godfather* films won a number of Oscars.

_____ **4.** Al Pacino and Robert De Niro are brilliant actors.

_____ **5.** Francis Ford Coppola directed the films.

_____ **6.** Several members of the Coppola family helped to make the films.

_____ **7.** Audiences all over the world will love *The Godfather* because it is exciting and unforgettable.

_____ **8.** The American Film Institute placed *The Godfather* on its list of the top ten greatest American movies.

_____ **9.** The *Godfather* movies have too much violence in them.

_____ 10. *Godfather II* was the best movie in the trilogy.

_____ 11. Film critics often include *The Godfather* in lists of their top ten favorite American films.

_____ 12. *Godfather III* was made in 1990.

Test Your Vocabulary

C. Choose the word that best completes each of the following sentences. Be sure to use the correct form of the word.

> admire   fictional   immigrate   revenge   take over
> change your mind   generation   patriarch   stereotype take place

1. John hopes to _____ his father's insurance business.

2. Mrs. Chen _____ to the United States when she was a child.

3. Cinderella is a _____ character.

4. I don't like the negative _____ of women in that movie.

5. The movie _____ in Mexico in the 1980s.

6. Everyone respected my Uncle Paul, who was the _____ of our family.

7. He wants to get _____ on the person who stole his car.

8. I _____ people who achieve their goals.

9. Four _____ of Hamiltons have lived in this house.

10. Let me know if you _____ about coming with me on Saturday.

D. Use context to figure out the meaning of the underlined word in each of the following sentences. Circle the best definition.

1. The rise and fall of the Corleone family is told in three films. The first film of the <u>trilogy</u>, *The Godfather*, is mainly the story of the aging Vito Corleone.
   a. movie theater   **b.** criminals   **c.** three films about the same subject

2. Vito has always wanted Michael to work in a legal <u>profession</u>.
   a. job   **b.** play   **c.** war

3. One story is about Michael's life as the <u>head</u> of the family business.
   a. brother   **b.** body   **c.** leader

4. Other critics <u>objected to</u> the violence shown in these movies.
   a. agreed with   **b.** disapproved of   **c.** hoped for

5. The films were <u>box office hits</u>, earning millions of dollars in movie theaters.
   a. highly praised **b.** famous   **c.** financially successful

Sharpen Your Vocabulary Skills

USING WORD MAPS

People learn and remember new information in different ways. When you are learning a new language, you need to learn many new vocabulary words. It can be difficult to remember the meanings of all the new words. One way to remember the meaning of new words is to make vocabulary word maps. A vocabulary word map is a diagram that helps you understand and remember the meaning of a word.

Follow these steps. Write the new word (or phrase) in the middle of the map. Then, fill in the rest of the map with a definition, a synonym, an antonym, a picture to help illustrate the new word, and a sentence that uses the word in context. Look at this example of a word map.

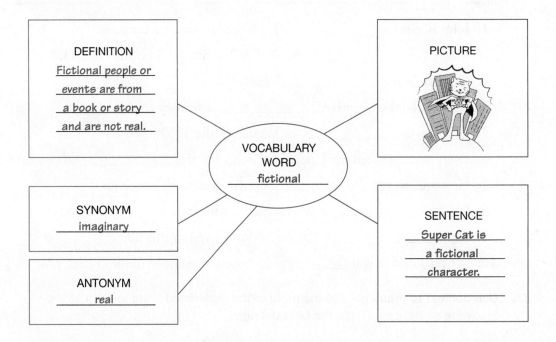

Choose two new words from the essay "*The Godfather:* A Movie Classic" that you want to learn and remember. Make a word map for each word. Share your word maps with a partner. Use them to teach your partner the meaning of the words.

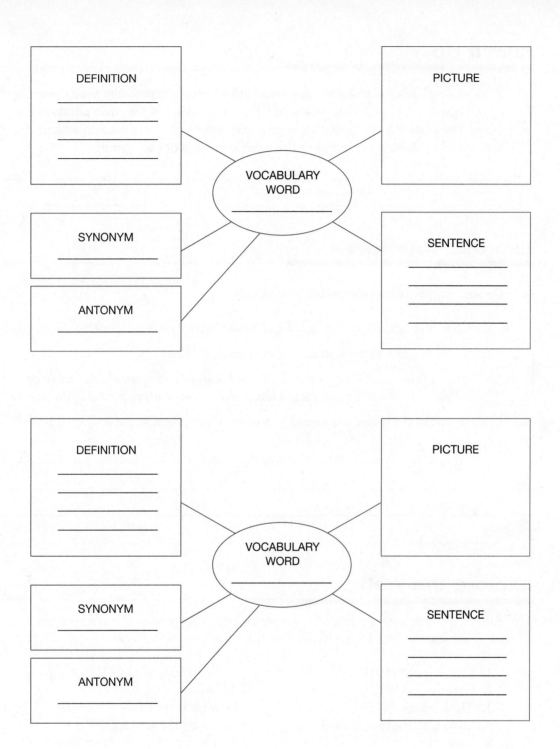

DEFINITION
_____
_____
_____
_____

PICTURE

VOCABULARY
WORD
_____

SYNONYM
_____

ANTONYM
_____

SENTENCE
_____
_____
_____
_____

DEFINITION
_____
_____
_____
_____

PICTURE

VOCABULARY
WORD
_____

SYNONYM
_____

ANTONYM
_____

SENTENCE
_____
_____
_____
_____

Sum It Up

Work in small groups. Imagine your friend asked you to explain the essay you just read, "*The Godfather:* A Movie Classic." First, write a list of the main points in the essay. Then use the list to explain in your own words what the reading was about. Take turns explaining the essay to the other members of your group.

_____

_____

Express Your Ideas

A. Discuss these questions in small groups.

1. What is your favorite movie? Why? What is your favorite scene in the movie?

2. Would you like to work in the movie industry? Why?

3. Do you think watching movies in English can help improve your language skills? How? What can you learn about American culture by watching movies?

B. Choose one of the questions above and write a paragraph about it.

_____

_____

_____

_____

Explore the Web

The American Film Institute recently announced the 100 greatest American movies of all time. Here are the first 15 movies on the list.

1. *Citizen Kane* (1941)
2. *Casablanca* (1942)
3. *The Godfather* (1972)
4. *Gone with the Wind* (1939)
5. *Lawrence of Arabia* (1962)
6. *The Wizard of Oz* (1939)
7. *The Graduate* (1967)
8. *On the Waterfront* (1954)
9. *Schindler's List* (1993)
10. *Singing in the Rain* (1952)
11. *It's a Wonderful Life* (1946)
12. *Sunset Boulevard* (1950)
13. *The Bridge on the River Kwai* (1957)
14. *Some Like It Hot* (1959)
15. *Star Wars* (1977)

Use the Internet to do some research about one of these movies. Write a paragraph about the movie. Include information about the story, actors, and director. Make copies of your paragraph and hand them out, or present the information in an oral report.

Become a Better Reader

Do your best to read the following text and answer the questions in three minutes. Then turn to page 169 to check your answers. Finally, turn to the chart on page 170 to keep track of your progress.

Charlie Chaplin: A Film Giant

1   Charlie Chaplin stands out as one of the most famous actors in international film history. He was not only a popular actor but also a writer and director. His movies are considered among the greatest classics of all time.

2   Chaplin had a difficult childhood in England. His father died when Charlie was a young child. His mother, who suffered from mental illness, was often unable to take care of the children. Charlie lived in orphanages and he was sometimes homeless and living on the streets. He tried to support himself and help his mother by singing and dancing in local shows.

3   Chaplin emigrated to the United States, where he soon became a star in Hollywood. Audiences loved his familiar character and laughed at the funny scenes in his comedies. Chaplin created his own movie studio and produced many successful films. His movies showed sympathy for the common working man and people who were unemployed. Because of Chaplin's sympathy for the poor and those less fortunate, some politicians accused him of being a communist.

4   Chaplin left the United States in the 1950s feeling angry at the political climate. He moved to Europe. However, near the end of his life, he returned to the United States to receive an honorary Academy Award. Many years after his death, Charlie Chaplin continues to be one of the best-loved men in the history of film.

1. Charlie Chaplin was
   a. a famous movie actor
   b. a writer and director
   c. a famous movie actor, and a writer and director

2. During his childhood, Charlie
   a. lived a comfortable life with his family
   b. sang and danced with his parents
   c. experienced many problems

3. After he moved to the United States, Chaplin
   a. worked for many years before he found a job as an actor
   b. was successful in making his own movies
   c. was often unemployed and homeless

4. Chaplin returned to the United States from Europe in order to
   a. receive an honorary award
   b. make more movies
   c. change the political climate of the United States

Have Some Fun

Read through the following newspaper section that tells what is going on in the city today. Discuss each event with a partner. Underline the facts and circle the opinions.

WHAT TO DO AROUND TOWN

1. Crafts Show and Festival—
Come help us celebrate our 25th anniversary. This year's festival will be bigger and better than ever! More than 75 artists and crafters will be present and selling their jewelry, pottery, glass, and paintings. Saturday, 9 A.M.–6 P.M. at the corner of Main Street and River Street. Rain date: June 14.

2. Free Concert—
Given by the Choral Singers, tonight at 7 P.M. in the Stone Harbor Concert Hall. Music written and composed by Swiss composer Frank Martin. This music is said to be one of the most beautiful pieces of music ever written.

3. Jazz in June Film Series—
Continuing our month-long tribute to jazz greats, Monday's film takes a look at the life and times of the great saxophonist Charlie Parker in *Celebrating! The Triumph of Charlie "Bird" Parker.* Saturday–Wednesday, 7:30 P.M., Museum Auditorium, 460 Avenue of the Arts. $10; senior citizens, students, and children $8.

4. Learn to play chess!—
Whether you are a beginner or an expert, come and enjoy playing chess with others who are interested in this fascinating game. Monday, 6–7 P.M., St. Louis Public Library.

5. River Festival—
From early morning to early evening, south of the city to north, people who live near the river will celebrate the importance of waterways in our lives on Sunday. We'll offer canoe trips, hikes, art exhibits, fishing competitions, boat rides, and a jazz concert! There'll be something for everyone in your family. Free. Call 555-1234 for more information.

6. Rhythms and Arts of Bali—
You won't need airline tickets to see and hear the wonderful music and dance of Bali. The Bali dance group will perform both traditional and contemporary works beginning at 7:30 tonight. Free, but tickets are required. Call 555-1234 to reserve your tickets.

CHAPTER 8

Read between the Lines
Making Inferences

Look at this painting by John Singer Sargent, a famous nineteenth-century portrait painter. Discuss it with a partner and then answer the questions that follow.

1. Based on what you see in the painting, which statements do you think are probably true about the two people? Check the boxes.

   ☐ They are meeting for the first time.   ☐ They have just played a game of tennis.

   ☐ They are wealthy.   ☐ They do not want to be in the painting.

2. What do you think the relationship is between the woman and the girl? Why?

3. How do you think the artist felt about the people in the painting?

4. When do you think this painting was done? A few years ago? Ten years ago? A hundred years ago? Why?

When you looked at the picture, you gathered information about the people based on what you saw in the painting and from your own personal knowledge. In other words, you made inferences. In the same way, you can use the information that is stated in a reading passage to make inferences about what is not stated.

Sharpen Your Reading Skills

MAKING INFERENCES

We make inferences all the time in our everyday lives. That is, we think something is true although we have no proof. Here is an example: If I tell you that I am going shopping for a birthday gift, you will probably guess that someone I know is having a birthday soon. I didn't tell you that someone I know is having a birthday soon. You made the inference based on the information I gave you.

Writers don't always state directly everything they want you to know. Often, they only suggest ideas by giving hints and clues. They expect you to figure out some things on your own. In other words, they want you to make inferences.

> An **inference** is an educated guess based on information in the reading. To make good inferences you should combine the clues in the reading with information you already know from your own life.

A. Circle the letter of the inference you can make based on the information.

Example

The young woman in the coffee shop kept checking the time on her watch and looking toward the door.

    a. She was afraid that her watch was broken.
    b. She was waiting for her coffee to cool.
    (**c.**) She was waiting for someone to arrive.

1. When the couple got out of their car, I saw that there were lots of cookie crumbs, a teddy bear, and a child safety seat in the back.

    a. The couple has a baby.
    b. The couple likes to eat cookies.
    c. The couple sells teddy bears.

2. Harry was sneezing and coughing a lot in class. His face was very pale.

    a. Harry was sick.
    b. Harry was trying to disturb the class.
    c. Harry was tired because he always stays up too late.

3. Outside the bank, a man in a blue shirt was gesturing with his arms and smiling as he spoke. Then he and the two men with him started to laugh.

   a. The man in the blue shirt was doing arm exercises.
   b. The man in the blue shirt was trying to hit the other men.
   c. The man in the blue shirt was telling a funny story.

4. When we went to visit Liz at her apartment last week, we noticed that she had maps on the walls, plane tickets to Japan on her table, and art objects from all over the world on her bookshelves.

   a. Liz is an artist.
   b. Liz is a travel agent.
   c. Liz enjoys traveling to different countries.

5. A woman has been standing in front of her house for ten minutes. She is looking in her pockets. She is emptying her purse. She seems annoyed.

   a. The woman can't find her keys.
   b. The woman doesn't like her purse.
   c. The woman has too many pockets.

B. **Work with a partner. Write an inference based on the information.**

1. Jorge put a plate of french fries with ketchup on the table and then went to buy a drink. When he returned, most of the french fries were gone, and Jorge noticed that his friend Carlos had ketchup on his mouth.

   _____

2. During the test, Rose waited until the teacher was answering a student's question. Then she quickly passed a small piece of paper to Jenny.

   _____

3. A reporter asked a politician how the government was going to provide social services if he cut taxes. The politician made a joke but didn't answer the question.

   _____

4. The door to the apartment flew open. A man raced out and ran over to the elevator. He waited for just a few seconds and then ran down the stairs.

   _____

5. In the opening scene of the movie, there were women wearing long dresses. There were horses on the road but no cars.

   _____

c. Read the following paragraphs and choose the best inference for each one.

1.   Sarah is a wonderful girl, but she is driving her mother crazy. Why? Because she talks constantly on her cell phone. Sarah thinks cell phones are the greatest invention of all time. She loves being able to stay in touch with all of her friends wherever she goes. However, Sarah's mother gets annoyed because she's tired of hearing the cell phone ring. She considers it an unwelcome interruption to family conversations. Now she has given Sarah two rules. First, no answering the cell phone during dinnertime. Two, no using the cell phone while driving. It is very dangerous to drive and talk on a cell phone. Sarah has promised to follow these rules, and she tries not to use her cell phone too much when she is with her mother.

What can you infer from the paragraph?
  a. Sarah's mother doesn't have a cell phone.
  b. Sarah's mother doesn't think cell phones are the greatest invention in the world.
  c. Sarah would rather talk on her cell phone than eat dinner with her family.

2.   Some people might complain about their jobs, but Janet never does. For three years, Janet has been a counselor at a state college. She helps hundreds of students choose and register for courses. Career counseling is her greatest interest. Janet enjoys finding websites about different occupations and helping students explore their options. Sometimes her day is very busy because lots of students come to the counseling office, especially at the beginning and end of each semester. Janet doesn't mind being busy, though. She loves working with people, giving advice, and finding solutions to problems.

What can you infer from the paragraph?
  a. Janet is looking for a new job.
  b. Janet likes her job.
  c. Janet doesn't like her job.

3.   Once upon a time there was a king named Midas who had a large fortune but was never satisfied. No matter how many riches he had, he always wanted more. One day he saved the life of a magic fish. In return, the fish said that he would give Midas one wish. Midas thought about which wish would give him the greatest fortune. Then he had his answer. Midas wished that everything he touched would turn to gold. First, Midas touched a flower and it turned to gold. Next, he touched a chair and it turned to gold. King Midas was so excited by his new ability to create enormous wealth. Suddenly, though, his daughter ran toward him. Midas had no time to stop her, and she, too, turned to gold. At that moment, Midas understood the true meaning of wealth and fortune.

What can you infer from the paragraph?
  a. Midas realized that wealth and fortune are not always good things.
  b. Midas realized that he wanted even more wealth and fortune.
  c. Midas wanted to give his daughter wealth and fortune.

4. Dave Thomas became a folk hero through his popular television commercials for Wendy's, the chain of fast-food restaurants he founded in 1969. He was always called "Dave" in the commercials, and was admired because of his honesty, good nature, and sense of humor. Wendy's, named after Dave's daughter, earned millions of dollars serving familiar fast foods such as hamburgers and fries, but also by offering other kinds of food such as baked potatoes, chili, and a variety of salads. The road to success wasn't always easy for Dave. He was adopted as an infant and dropped out of school at age fifteen. He considered dropping out of school to be his biggest mistake in life. After earning a fortune through Wendy's, Dave decided to finish high school. Dave devoted his later years to the Dave Thomas Foundation for Adoption, an organization he founded to increase awareness of adoption and make the process more affordable. Dave died in 2002, and today he is remembered for his honesty and old-fashioned values.

What can you infer from the paragraph?
   a. Dave believed that education was important.
   b. Most people would rather eat chili than hamburgers.
   c. Wendy's is the most popular fast-food chain in the United States.

5. Rosa and Harry are looking for an apartment. They are going to get married next month, and they want to move into a nice place for their new home. However, finding an apartment isn't easy. Many of the apartments listed in the newspaper are too expensive, and the cheaper ones all have problems. The first apartment they looked at was too small, a studio with just one tiny room and a bathroom. The next apartment was very dirty and in bad condition. Everything seemed to be broken or falling apart. The third one was located on top of a restaurant and was too noisy. Rosa and Harry are going to look at another apartment tonight, and they hope that this one will be the perfect place.

What can you infer from the paragraph?
   a. Rosa and Harry are too critical about the apartments they look at.
   b. Rosa and Harry disagree about the kind of apartment they should rent.
   c. Rosa and Harry are looking for a clean, quiet, moderately priced apartment.

D. Work with a partner. Make an inference based on the information in each of the following paragraphs. Then, compare your inferences with the inferences of another pair of students.

1. Catherine II was a German princess who became the empress of Russia in 1762. Catherine expanded Russia during her rule to include parts of the Ottoman Empire, Poland, and Siberia. In addition, she admired the culture of the West and encouraged interest in the arts, literature, science, and politics. She also built schools and hospitals, established the first school for girls, and gave women important political jobs. By the time of her death in 1796, she had turned Russia into a world power. For these reasons and for her success in modernizing the administration, she is remembered as Catherine the Great.

Inference: _____

(Continued on next page.)

2. The world's population has been increasing at a fast rate during the past few centuries. Scientists estimate that for thousands of years, the human population grew slowly. After 1700, there was a steady increase in population because of better agricultural methods, improved sanitation, and advances in the field of medicine. The population has continued to grow at a fast pace. It took hundreds of thousands of years for the world's population to total about 1 billion in 1800. It reached 2 billion in just one more century and has rapidly grown to more than 5 billion today. Serious problems have resulted from this sudden population explosion. People are using up the world's natural resources at a faster rate than they can develop, forests are disappearing, and pollution is increasing. As the world's population continues to increase sharply, these issues must be addressed for the safety and health of future generations.

Inference: _____

 TIP To make an inference:

1. Look for clues as you read.
2. Think about what you know from other experiences in your own life.
3. Put together clues in the reading with what you already know.

Test Your Skills

Read each of the following paragraphs and answer the four questions that follow. The first question is about the main idea of the passage. The second and third questions test your understanding of details in the passage. The fourth question asks you to make an inference.

A. Every year, the Nobel Committee gives the Nobel Peace Prize to a group or individual who has promoted world peace. Recently, it gave the Nobel Peace Prize to the United Nations and its top official, Secretary General Kofi Annan. The committee said that the only road to world "peace and cooperation goes by way of the United Nations." Kofi Annan also received special recognition for "bringing new life to the organization." Annan was born in the African country of Ghana and studied at universities in Ghana, Switzerland, and the United States. He became secretary general of the United Nations in 1997. Since then, he has worked hard to solve problems such as AIDS and world hunger, and he has tried to resolve conflicts between countries. He surely has a difficult and challenging job, but many people have praised Kofi Annan because of his commitment to world peace.

1. The main idea of the passage is that
   a. the Nobel Peace Prize is given every year
   b. the United Nations won the Nobel Peace Prize recently
   c. the United Nations and Kofi Annan won the Nobel Peace Prize because of their efforts to promote world peace

2. The Nobel Committee honored Kofi Annan because he
   a. studied in three countries
   b. brought new life to the United Nations
   c. had a difficult job

3. The secretary general is
   a. the top official of the United Nations
   b. the top official of the Nobel Prize Committee
   c. anyone who works at the United Nations

4. We can infer that in 2001, Kofi Annan
   a. solved all conflicts between countries
   b. solved the problems of AIDS and world hunger
   c. was still working on serious world problems

B.   Anyone who has trouble choosing a name for a baby can find help in a government website. The Social Security Administration (SSA), a government organization that deals with records of job earnings and retirement benefits, provides a list of the most popular baby names. These are the names that appear most often on applications for babies' social security cards. In 2003, the favorite name for a girl was Emily, and for a boy, Jacob. The second most popular name for a girl was Emma, and for a boy, Michael. Michael was at the top of the list for over thirty years, from 1964 to 1998. Names beginning with the letter A have been popular lately, with Alexis, Ashley, and Abigail for girls, and Andrew for boys all appearing in the top 10 list. Each year, the SSA website provides the top 1,000 favorite names in the United States as a whole and also has lists for individual states.

1. The main idea of the passage is that
   a. parents have trouble choosing names for their children
   b. the government provides a list of the most popular baby names
   c. Emily and Jacob were the most popular names for babies in 2003

2. The popular names on the SSA list come from applications for
   a. jobs
   b. retirement benefits
   c. social security cards

3. The Social Security Administration is
   a. a private organization that helps people find jobs
   b. a government organization that deals with job earnings and retirement benefits
   c. a government organization that chooses the best names for babies

4. We can conclude from the passage that Americans
   a. love the name Michael
   b. are too lazy to think of their own names for babies
   c. like the name Emily more than Jacob

C. Eric opened his wallet and sighed. There were only a few dollars in it. A week ago, Eric cashed a paycheck from his part-time job and got several hundred dollars. Where did all his money go? Eric couldn't figure out what had happened to it all. He tried to remember where he had spent money during the past week. On Saturday, he went to a movie with his girlfriend and bought tickets, drinks, and a giant-sized popcorn. His girlfriend doesn't eat much, but Eric likes to snack. He also bought lunch every day in the cafeteria, ate dinner in restaurants a few times, and bought some CDs. He wasn't sure what happened to the rest of the money. Somehow, it all seemed to disappear. Eric was afraid to ask his parents for money since they had already given him some last month. Oh, well. He decided not to worry about it. Maybe he could borrow some money from his girlfriend.

1. The main idea of this passage is that
   a. Eric has only a few dollars in his wallet
   b. Eric is confused about how he spent so much money this past week
   c. Eric plans to borrow money from his girlfriend

2. Eric spent a lot of his money on
   a. food and entertainment
   b. his girlfriend
   c. his parents

3. In the fifth sentence, to *figure out* means
   a. to keep a secret about something
   b. to understand something after thinking about it
   c. to need something very badly

4. We can infer that
   a. Eric has a wonderful relationship with his girlfriend
   b. Eric's parents will be happy to give him as much money as he needs
   c. Eric is not very careful about managing his money

Be an Active Reader

BEFORE YOU READ

A. Look at the map. Can you locate Nuweiba?

B. In small groups, discuss these questions.

    1. Have you ever gone fishing? Do you like to fish?

    2. Is fishing a popular activity in your hometown?

    3. Have you ever seen a dolphin?

    4. Would you like to swim with a dolphin?

C. Read the title of the article on page 158 and look at the picture. Can you guess what the article will be about? Think of three topics that might be discussed in the article.

    1. _____   **3.** _____

    2. _____

Vocabulary Preview

The words in the box are boldfaced in the article. Work with a partner and do the exercise that follows.

Words to Watch

buddies	dive	social	companionship
spot	cautiously	marine biologist	content

D. Match the words and phrases in the left column with the correct definitions in the right column. If you need help, read the sentence in the article where the word or phrase appears and think about how it is used.

    ____ **1.** companionship   **a.** with care

    ____ **2.** social   **b.** a friendly relationship

    ____ **3.** cautiously   **c.** to jump into the water, usually headfirst

    ____ **4.** marine biologist   **d.** good friends

    ____ **5.** buddies   **e.** to notice something that is difficult to see

    ____ **6.** content (*adj.*)   **f.** likes to live as part of a group

    ____ **7.** spot (*v.*)   **g.** a scientist who studies sea animals

    ____ **8.** dive (*v.*)   **h.** satisfied because you have what you want or need

Set a Purpose

You are going to read a story about a fisherman who makes friends with a dolphin. What do you want to find out about the fisherman and the dolphin?

_____

_____

AS YOU READ

As you read the article, complete the chart on the opposite page with details from the article.

Swimming **Buddies**

Making Friends

1 Five years ago, a fisherman named Abeidalla Mekiten **spotted** a big, gray animal swimming near his fishing boat. It was a bottlenose dolphin.

2 Over the next few days, Mekiten, who lives in Nuweiba, Egypt, watched the dolphin patiently. He decided to **dive** into the water for a closer look. To Mekiten's surprise the dolphin didn't swim away. Instead she looked at him **cautiously**. Day after day the two swam together. Mekiten named the dolphin Olin. Then one morning, Olin let the fisherman touch her. A long friendship began between the wild, free dolphin and the young man.

Social Animals

3 Dolphins do not like to be alone. They are **social** animals that like to live with others.

Most dolphins live in family groups of up to twelve members. The groups are called pods. Often, many pods swim together to form larger groups of hundreds of dolphins. Occasionally one dolphin is forced out of its pod by the other dolphins in the pod. "Those that are thrown out may not want to be alone," says Oz Goffman, a **marine biologist** (a scientist who studies animals that live in the water) at the University of Haifa in Israel. He studies the friendship between Mekiten and Olin. A single dolphin may be lonely. It might "replace the **companionship** of the pod with that of human beings." Such behavior may explain why Olin, completely free to swim away, has stayed near Nuweiba. Once in a while, Olin joins a passing dolphin pod for a few days, but she always returns to the waters off Nuweiba.

A Baby Is Born

4 During a visit with other dolphins, Olin became pregnant. A year later she gave birth to a male calf. Now Mekiten plays with mother and baby. Says Goffman, "Human-dolphin friendships are rare, but this is obviously a friendship Olin wants, or she would leave." So far Olin seems **content** to stay.

5 Tourists from all over the world now visit Nuweiba for a chance to swim alongside the wild dolphin. They must be careful not to get too close, because Olin is not always as friendly with strangers as she is with Mekiten.

Details

gave birth to a male calf

became friends with a wild dolphin

live in family groups called pods

studies the friendship between Mekiten and Olin

became pregnant

a fisherman from Nuweiba, Egypt

is not always friendly to strangers

social animals

a marine biologist

always returns to the waters off Nuweiba

Topic	Details
Abeidalla Mekiten	1. _a fisherman from Nuweiba, Egypt_ 2. _____
Olin	1. _____ 2. _____ 3. _____ 4. _____
Dr. Oz Goffman	1. _____ 2. _____
bottlenose dolphins	1. _____ 2. _____

AFTER YOU READ

After you have read "Swimming Buddies," complete the following exercises.

Check Your Comprehension

See how much you can remember from "Swimming Buddies." If you are not sure of the answer, you can refer to the article.

A. True or False? Write T (True) or F (False) next to each of the following statements. If a statement is false, correct it to make it true.

____ **1.** Mekiten and Olin are friends.

____ **2.** Tourists come to Nuweiba to swim with Olin.

____ **3.** Most dolphins live in family groups called pods.

____ **4.** Sometimes hundreds of dolphins swim together.

____ **5.** Olin gave birth to a male calf.

____ **6.** Dolphins like to be alone.

____ **7.** Oz Goffman is a fisherman.

____ **8.** Dolphins are social animals.

____ **9.** Dolphins are often forced out of their pods.

____**10.** Human-dolphin friendships are rare.

____**11.** Only scientists visit Nuweiba for a chance to swim with Olin.

____**12.** Olin is not permitted to swim away.

B. Make Inferences. Put a check next to the statements that you can infer from reading "Swimming Buddies."

____ **1.** Mekiten is a good swimmer.

____ **2.** Olin likes Mekiten.

____ **3.** Dolphins rarely have twins.

____ **4.** Sometimes Olin is friendly to strangers.

____ **5.** Nuweiba is the only place tourists can go to swim with dolphins.

____ **6.** Pods of dolphins swim together for protection.

____ **7.** Olin prefers to be in the waters off Nuweiba.

____ **8.** The University of Haifa has a famous marine biology department.

____ **9.** When Mekiten first saw Olin, he expected the dolphin to swim away.

____**10.** Most dolphins live in the wild.

____**11.** Olin's baby is not very friendly.

Test Your Vocabulary

C. Choose the word or phrase that best completes each of the following sentences. Be sure to use the correct form of the word or phrase.

> buddies   companionship   dive   once in a while
> cautiously   content   marine biologist   social

1. Jane is my best friend. We've been _____ for years.

2. I usually walk to school, but _____ I take a bus.

3. Ants are _____ animals that live in large groups.

4. Jason is _____ to sit at home and watch TV every night.

5. If you are interested in the behavior of animals that live in the water, you should think about becoming a _____.

6. The water looks inviting. I can't wait to _____ in and go swimming.

7. Stan lives alone but is not lonely. He enjoys the _____ of his pets.

8. There is a lot of traffic on this road. You should drive _____ and watch where you are going.

D. Each of the following words from the article has more than one meaning. Use a dictionary to find the definition that fits the word as it is used in the sentence. Write the definition on the line.

1. Such behavior may explain why Olin, completely <u>free</u> to swim away, has stayed near Nuweiba.

   free: _____

2. Tourists from all over the world now visit Nuweiba for a <u>chance</u> to swim alongside the wild dolphin.

   chance: _____

3. Five years ago, a fisherman named Abeidalla Mekiten <u>spotted</u> a big, gray animal swimming near his fishing boat.

   spotted: _____

4. Once in a while, Olin joins a <u>passing</u> dolphin pod for a few days, but she always returns to the waters off Nuweiba.

   passing: _____

5. "Human-dolphin friendships are <u>rare</u>, but this is obviously a friendship Olin wants, or she would leave."

   rare: _____

E. Make Word Maps. Choose four new words you want to learn and remember from "Swimming Buddies." Make a word map for each one.

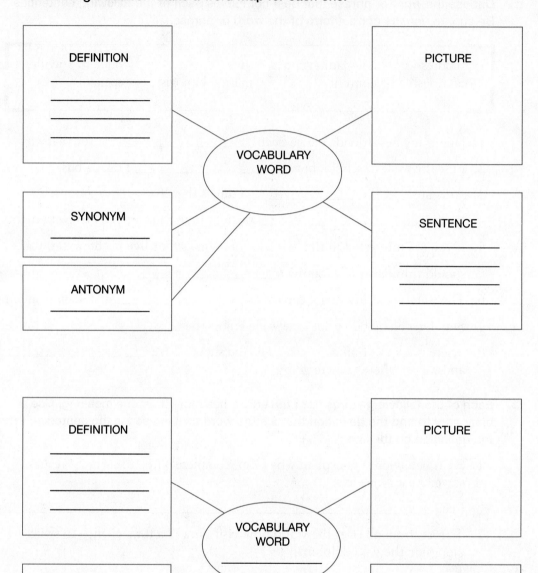

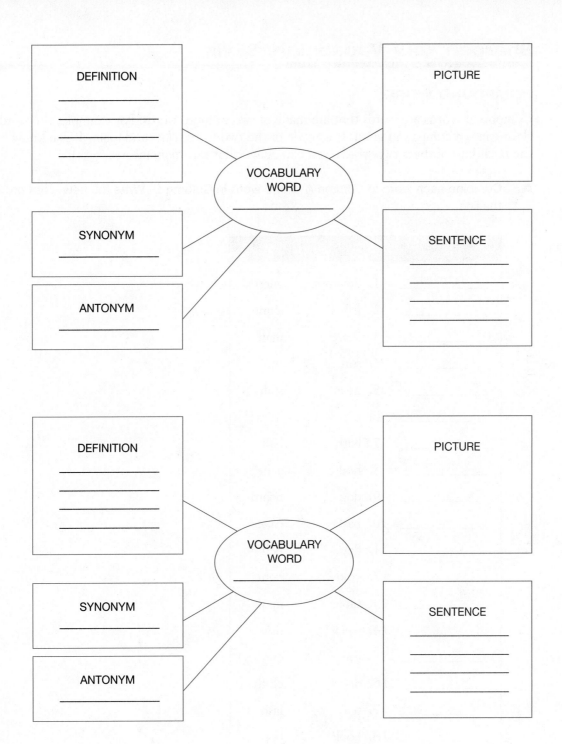

DEFINITION
_____
_____
_____
_____

PICTURE

VOCABULARY
WORD
_____

SYNONYM
_____

ANTONYM
_____

SENTENCE
_____
_____
_____
_____

DEFINITION
_____
_____
_____
_____

PICTURE

VOCABULARY
WORD
_____

SYNONYM
_____

ANTONYM
_____

SENTENCE
_____
_____
_____
_____

Sharpen Your Vocabulary Skills

COMPOUND WORDS

Compound words are words that are made of two or more words. For example, the word *classroom* is a compound word. It is made of the two words *class* and *room*. If you know the meanings of these two words, you can guess what *classroom* means.

A. Combine each word in Column A with a word in Column B. Write the new word on the line.

		A	B
downstairs	1.	down	guest
_____	2.	fisher	shine
_____	3.	skate	man
_____	4.	sun	tub
_____	5.	head	stairs
_____	6.	cup	house
_____	7.	bath	ball
_____	8.	house	ache
_____	9.	dog	board
_____	10.	basket	cake
_____	11.	day	bell
_____	12.	gold	light
_____	13.	table	mail
_____	14.	week	fish
_____	15.	eye	end
_____	16.	door	cloth
_____	17.	tea	lash
_____	18.	book	pot
_____	19.	air	case

B. Underline the compound words in this paragraph from Chapter 6.

The snowplows in Toronto were very busy this weekend. The snow started falling on Friday night. It was light at first, but by Saturday morning, there were 10 inches of the white stuff on the ground. Heavy snow continued to fall, and at 5 P.M., there were over 2 feet of snow. At 7 P.M., major roads were closed, and soon the airport was closed, too. It didn't stop snowing until late Sunday morning. This was the worst snowstorm of the winter.

Sum It Up

Work in small groups. Imagine your friend asked you to explain the article you just read, "Swimming Buddies." First, write a list of the main points in the article. Then use the list to explain in your own words what the reading was about. Take turns explaining the article to the other members of your group.

_____

_____

_____

_____

Express Your Ideas

A. Discuss these questions in small groups.

1. Would you like to visit Nuweiba and go swimming with Olin? Would you be excited or afraid?

2. Are you interested in the behavior of dolphins or any other marine animal? Would you like to be a marine biologist?

3. Do you like to visit other places as a tourist? Do you like it when tourists visit your hometown?

B. Choose one of the questions above and write a paragraph about it.

_____

_____

_____

_____

_____

Explore the Web

Work with a partner. Use the Internet to do some research about the behavior of other marine animals such as whales, seals, stingrays, and sea otters. Choose the one that is the most interesting to you, and then do one of the following.

1. Draw or find a picture of the animal and take notes about its behavior. Show the picture to the class and share your information in a short oral presentation.

2. Write a paragraph about the animal you chose. Make copies of your paragraph and hand them out to your classmates. Discuss the animals and decide which one has the most interesting behavior.

Become a Better Reader

Do your best to read the following text and answer the questions in three minutes. Then turn to page 169 to check your answers. Finally, turn to the chart on page 170 to keep track of your progress.

The Manatee: An Unusual Animal

1   Visitors to Florida and other places throughout the Caribbean and Gulf of Mexico may be able to see an unusual animal called the manatee. Manatees are large mammals that live in the water, usually along the coast or in lakes and rivers. They are about 8–15 feet (2.5–4.5 meters) long, and some weigh as much as 1,500 pounds (700 kilograms).

2   Although manatees are huge animals, they move slowly through the water and do not attack other animals. They cannot live in deep water because they live on plants that grow in shallow water. They need to live close to land in order to eat. They also need to come up to the surface of the water to breathe. For this reason, it is often possible to see manatees. In addition, they swim slowly.

3   Manatees have no natural enemies among other animals. However, they are in danger of becoming extinct, or dying out as a species. Boats are a danger to manatees. Because manatees are so slow, it's difficult for them to swim away from speeding boats, and they are often injured or killed when boats hit them. There are now laws to protect the manatee, and marine biologists are trying to help them to survive. The survival of the manatee has become a popular cause, especially in Florida, which has the largest population of manatees.

1. Manatees live
   a. in the middle of the ocean, far away from land
   b. in water that is near land
   c. only in Florida

2. A danger to manatees is
   a. larger animals
   b. water plants
   c. fast-moving boats

3. Manatees weigh
   a. about 1,500 pounds
   b. about 700 pounds
   c. about 2.5 to 4.5 pounds

4. The population of manatees is
   a. getting larger all over the Caribbean
   b. in danger of dying out
   c. moving to the Gulf of Mexico

Have Some Fun

Tourists travel all over the world to have real-life experiences with wild animals. Look at the travel ads. Talk to a partner about which experiences you would like to have.

SWIM WITH DOLPHINS in Nassau

Enjoy the experience of a lifetime! Take a 25-minute boat ride, with great views of Nassau Harbour and surrounding islands, to the beautiful Blue Lagoon Island. You'll be able to dive into the water for a swim with the dolphins—one of the ocean's most fascinating and intelligent animals. You will have the chance to touch, kiss, feed, and even dance with these lovable mammals.

Price $145
Includes round-trip boat ride to Blue Lagoon Island.

GO SNOWMOBILING IN CANADA

Visit Algonquin Park, Ontario—a world-famous "Wilderness Park." Go snowmobiling in the beautiful park and you will have a good chance of seeing wild animals like moose, deer, beaver, or even wolves! You will pass by several beaver dams (now frozen over), so keep your camera within easy reach!

TAKE A RIDE ON AN ELEPHANT IN ZIMBABWE

Take a two-hour ride through the bush on an elephant! Learn about these amazing animals and have a special experience with one. After the ride, enjoy a delicious lunch by the lake and watch the elephants play in the water.

Take a class survey. Which trip was the most popular?

Pretend you are having one of the animal experiences in the travel ads. Use the space below to write a postcard to a friend.

Dear _____ ,

_____

_____

_____

_____

_____

_____

_____

84 Maple Street

Hawthorne, NY 10532

See you soon,

_____

Become a Better Reader

CORRECT ANSWERS				
CHAPTER 1	1. c	2. b	3. a	4. c
CHAPTER 2	1. b	2. c	3. a	4. a
CHAPTER 3	1. c	2. c	3. b	4. c
CHAPTER 4	1. b	2. c	3. a	4. c
CHAPTER 5	1. a	2. b	3. b	4. c
CHAPTER 6	1. a	2. c	3. b	4. a
CHAPTER 7	1. c	2. c	3. b	4. a
CHAPTER 8	1. b	2. c	3. a	4. b

Become a Better Reader

KEEP TRACK OF YOUR PROGRESS

	NUMBER OF CORRECT ANSWERS			
	1	2	3	4
CHAPTER 1				
CHAPTER 2				
CHAPTER 3				
CHAPTER 4				
CHAPTER 5				
CHAPTER 6				
CHAPTER 7				
CHAPTER 8				